PLAN TO STAY™

PEACHTREE CITY LIBRARY
201 Willowbend Road
Peachtree City, GA 30269-1623
Phone: 770-631-2520
Fax: 770-631-2522

Avi

WHO WROTE THAT?

Avi

Margaret Speaker Yuan

Foreword by
Kyle Zimmer

CHELSEA HOUSE
PUBLISHERS
A Haights Cross Communications Company ®
Philadelphia

CHELSEA HOUSE PUBLISHERS

VP, NEW PRODUCT DEVELOPMENT Sally Cheney
DIRECTOR OF PRODUCTION Kim Shinners
CREATIVE MANAGER Takeshi Takahashi
MANUFACTURING MANAGER Diann Grasse

STAFF FOR AVI

EXECUTIVE EDITOR Matt Uhler
EDITORIAL ASSISTANT Sarah Sharpless
PRODUCTION EDITOR Noelle Nardone
PHOTO EDITOR Sarah Bloom
SERIES DESIGNER Keith Trego
LAYOUT 21st Century Publishing and Communications, Inc.

http://www.chelseahouse.com

A Haights Cross Communications ⟍ Company®

First Printing

1 3 5 7 9 8 6 4 2

Library of Congress Cataloging-in-Publication Data

Speaker-Yuan, Margaret.
   Avi/Margaret Speaker Yuan.
     p. cm.—(Who wrote that?)
   Includes bibliographical references.
   ISBN 0-7910-8230-X (alk. paper)
  1. Avi, 1937– 2. Authors, American—20th century—Biography. 3. Children's
stories—Authorship. I Title. II. Series.
PS3551. V5Z83 2004
813'.54—dc22
                                                              2004023883

Table of Contents

FOREWORD BY
KYLE ZIMMER
PRESIDENT, FIRST BOOK

HUMANITY IS POWERED by stories. From our earliest days as thinking beings, we employed every available tool to tell each other stories. We danced, drew pictures on the walls of our caves, spoke, and sang. All of this extraordinary effort was designed to entertain, recount the news of the day, explain natural occurrences—and then gradually to build religious and cultural traditions and establish the common bonds and continuity that eventually formed civilizations. Stories are the most powerful force in the universe; they are the primary element that has distinguished our evolutionary path.

Our love of the story has not diminished with time. Enormous segments of societies are devoted to the art of storytelling. Book sales in the United States alone topped $26 billion last year; movie studios spend fortunes to create and promote stories; and the news industry is more pervasive in its presence than ever before.

There is no mystery to our fascination. Great stories are magic. They can introduce us to new cultures, or remind us of the nobility and failures of our own, inspire us to greatness or scare us to death; but above all, stories provide human insight on a level that is unavailable through any other source. In fact, stories connect each of us to the rest of humanity not just in our own time, but also throughout history.

This special magic of books is the greatest treasure that we can hand down from generation to generation. In fact, that spark in a child that comes from books became the motivation for the creation of my organization, First Book, a national literacy program with a simple mission: to provide new books to the most disadvantaged children. At present, First Book has been at work in hundreds of communities for over a decade. Every year children in need receive millions of books through our organization and millions more are provided through dedicated literacy institutions across the United States and around the world. In addition, groups of people dedicate themselves tirelessly to working with children to share reading and stories in every imaginable setting from schools to the streets. Of course, this Herculean effort serves many important goals. Literacy translates to productivity and employability in life and many other valid and even essential elements. But at the heart of this movement are people who love stories, love to read, and want desperately to ensure that no one misses the wonderful possibilities that reading provides.

When thinking about the importance of books, there is an overwhelming urge to cite the literary devotion of great minds. Some have written of the magnitude of the importance of literature. Amy Lowell, an American poet, captured the concept when she said, "Books are more than books. They are the life, the very heart and core of ages past, the reason why men lived and worked and died, the essence and quintessence of their lives." Others have spoken of their personal obsession with books, as in Thomas Jefferson's simple statement: "I live for books." But more compelling, perhaps, is the almost instinctive excitement in children for books and stories.

Throughout my years at First Book, I have heard truly extraordinary stories about the power of books in the lives of children. In one case, a homeless child, who had been bounced from one location to another, later resurfaced— and the only possession that he had fought to keep was the book he was given as part of a First Book distribution months earlier. More recently, I met a child who, upon receiving the book he wanted, flashed a big smile and said, "This is my big chance!" These snapshots reveal the true power of books and stories to give hope and change lives.

As these children grow up and continue to develop their love of reading, they will owe a profound debt to those volunteers who reached out to them—a debt that they may repay by reaching out to spark the next generation of readers. But there is a greater debt owed by all of us— a debt to the storytellers, the authors, who have bound us together, inspired our leaders, fueled our civilizations, and helped us put our children to sleep with their heads full of images and ideas.

WHO WROTE THAT? is a series of books dedicated to introducing us to a few of these incredible individuals. While we have almost always honored stories, we have not uniformly honored storytellers. In fact, some of the most important authors have toiled in complete obscurity throughout their lives or have been openly persecuted for the uncomfortable truths that they have laid before us. When confronted with the magnitude of their written work or perhaps the daily grind of our own, we can forget that writers are people. They struggle through the same daily indignities and dental appointments, and they experience the intense joy and bottomless despair that many of us do. Yet somehow they rise above it all to deliver a powerful thread that connects us all. It is a rare honor to have the opportunity that these books provide to share the lives of these extraordinary people. Enjoy.

Avi grew up in a typical Brooklyn brownstone home similar to these buildings. Built in the mid-nineteenth century, the brownstones were, and still are, large and comfortable homes. Avi's father, Dr. Wortis, practiced psychiatry on the first floor, while the family lived on the upper three floors.

1

A Childhood of Books and Stories

A MEETING THAT CHANGED AVI'S LIFE

AVI'S HIGH SCHOOL English teacher, Mr. Stillman, called Avi's parents. Avi was in his second year at Elizabeth Irwin High, a small private school in New York City. "My English teacher called my folks and told them I was truly the worst student he had ever had," Avi wrote.[1] Avi was in danger of flunking out of high school, Mr. Stillman reported to Dr. and Mrs. Wortis. Something needed to be done.

Avi had already failed at another high school. Shy and small for his age, Avi had spent his first quarter of ninth grade at

Peter Stuyvesant High School, a huge, overcrowded public school that his brother Henry attended. Avi's first report card showed all Fs. He had failed every course. His parents transferred him to Elizabeth Irwin, where students received specialized, individual attention. Avi loved his new school, but despite the nurturing academic atmosphere, he continued to do poorly. By his sophomore year, he was in danger of failing again. Mr. Stillman recommended a private tutor who would work with him to improve his writing skills.

The first meeting with Avi's new tutor, Ella Ratner, changed his life. During high school, Avi had written constantly, but no one had ever recognized his creativity. He was so nervous about criticism that when he occasionally showed something that he had written to his classmates, he pretended it was the work of someone else. He pretended that he had copied another writer's material down in his handwriting. He never acknowledged the work as his own original ideas or writing.

Ella Ratner was different. "She spent that first meeting with me talking about my work," he said.[2] It was the first time anyone had ever sat down with him and talked about what he was trying to say instead of correcting the mechanics of his writing. She commented, "You're very interesting. You have lots of interesting ideas. If you wrote better, people would know that."[3] For a teenage boy who had never

Did you know...

Avi has never revealed his full name for book publication. He uses only the nickname "Avi" that his twin sister gave him as a baby.

before been recognized as a creative, interesting person, Mrs. Ratner's comments were a revelation. Before that day, people—his teachers, his parents, his classmates—had criticized his spelling or his handwriting. Mrs. Ratner's comments were about the ideas in Avi's writing.

"See, the way she phrased it was so wonderful," wrote Avi. "It was if you wrote well, then other people would understand you. Not you will understand yourself. This was not journal keeping, this was a way of communicating . . . She changed what the whole notion of writing was for me. Writing is not self-expression, it's a system of communicating."[4]

After their first meeting, Mrs. Ratner worked with him every day. "[She] not only taught me writing basics, but also instilled in me the conviction that I wanted to be a writer myself. Perhaps it was stubbornness. It was generally agreed that was one thing I could not possibly do."[5] With her help, Avi's writing improved enough to allow him not only to finish high school, but to go on to college.

BOYHOOD IN A BROWNSTONE HOUSE

Avi was born in Manhattan on December 23, 1937, one of a set of twins. His twin sister Emily called him Avi when she began to speak. The nickname stuck, and Avi used it exclusively, to the point that he has never used his given name for book publication.

Both of Avi's parents were the children of Jewish immigrants from different parts of Europe. Avi's father, Joseph Wortis, was a psychiatrist. His mother, Helen Zunser Wortis, was a social worker. Joseph and Helen met in high school. They went to the same college and were married after graduation. Avi had one brother, Henry, who was born in 1935.

When Avi was six months old, his family moved into a brownstone house in a quiet neighborhood in Brooklyn.

Brownstone houses—solid, large, comfortable houses built of brownish-red sandstone—were a fixture of New York City residential architecture. Avi's house, one of a row of houses dating back almost a century, was to be the Wortis family's home throughout Avi's school years. The first floor became Dr. Wortis's medical office, where he conducted his psychiatry practice and saw his patients. The family lived in the upper three stories of the house. When they were little, the children all shared a room on the third floor.

A number of relatives, including uncles, aunts, cousins, and both sets of grandparents, lived near Avi's house. Often the extended family shared meals and holidays. Avi's parents were not religious. They never attended religious services; however, they did follow some of the traditions of Judaism, more for their cultural significance than as religious celebrations. For instance, the Wortis family lit candles on Hanukkah in order to remember their Jewish heritage, but they always had a Christmas tree. Avi's maternal grandfather refused to enter the house when there was a Christmas tree present. When he came to visit in the winter, they took the Christmas tree outside until after he left.[6]

Avi's father in particular treated the religious traditions of Judaism lightly. During Passover, when the religious stories of the holiday were told and prayers were said over dinner, Dr. Wortis sometimes slipped a different book inside his copy of the Haggadah, the book that contained the night's stories and prayers. He would read his own book rather than pay attention to the rituals of the holiday. In an interview, Avi said that this behavior was his father's idea of a joke. Avi grew up as an atheist, one who does not believe in God in any form.[7]

Family life for Avi included a rich tradition of writing and storytelling. One of his great-grandfathers was a *bachen*, or folk bard, who told stories in Yiddish (a dialect that is a mixture of medieval German, Hebrew, and Aramaic languages) at Jewish weddings. Avi's grandfather also told tales in Yiddish. His delivery was so dramatic that young children, Avi included, who did not speak Yiddish, would laugh out loud at the punch lines of jokes they did not understand.

Family gatherings were not limited to marriages and celebrations. Surrounding the dinner table at Avi's house would be grandparents, aunts, uncles, and cousins as well as his parents, brother, and sister. The dinner conversations were lively, as the family debated many of the important social issues of the day. Their political orientation was progressive and liberal. They believed in equality for women, integration of all races, and fair treatment of workers. Discussions around the dinner table included many wide-ranging topics, from economics to literature to music to many other cultural issues.

For entertainment, the Wortis family played games, read books, and listened to the radio. Most families in the 1940s did not watch television, for while television had been invented in 1925, it was not yet in widespread public use. Transistors were not invented until 1948, so small, portable radios were years in the future. In the evening, families gathered in the living room around the radio, which often stood over two feet tall and weighted fifteen to twenty pounds. Programs broadcast on the radio included the news, comedies, dramas, and live broadcasts of sporting events.

Radio announcers gave dramatic descriptions of horse races and baseball games. The words, "She's coming down the stretch, ahead by a nose," or calls of "SAFE!" "OUT!" or "STRIKE THREE!" helped listeners imagine the action of their favorite sports. Avi and his brother Henry enjoyed

In the 1940s, the family radio was the focal point of entertainment in the home. Much like television today, radio broadcasts included news, comedies, dramas, and live sporting events. The title of Avi's book, "Who Was that Masked Man, Anyway?" came from one such radio program, **The Lone Ranger,** *a program that Avi enjoyed as a boy.*

listening to broadcasts of the Brooklyn Dodgers, their local baseball team.

The boys occasionally attended Dodgers games at the Brooklyn ballpark, Ebbets Field. Their father, however, demonstrated his lack of understanding of their interest in baseball when he turned down a gift from one of his patients. The patient, who was married to a Dodgers executive, offered a set of season tickets to Dr. Wortis. Dr. Wortis refused the tickets, saying he would not be interested in attending the games. He did not consider, according to Avi, whether or not his children would have enjoyed the games.[8]

Radio shows were not limited to sporting events. Avi and his family listened to dramas acted out completely by voice, or comedies where sound or voice effects added to the humor. Jack Benny was one of the most popular stand-up comedians. His off-key violin music enlivened the shows. Comedian Jack Allen, hearing the terrible scratchy notes, commented that when Benny played the violin, it sounded like the catgut strings were still in the cat.

News programs on the radio often presented live broadcasts of speeches and the "fireside chats" of then-President, Franklin Delano Roosevelt. Roosevelt had been elected president in 1932, long before Avi was born. President Roosevelt's policies were seen as the key to ending the Great Depression.

The Great Depression was a period in the late 1920s and 1930s. People did not have money to buy manufactured goods, so factories closed and put people out of work. Many who lost their jobs could not find new ones. People found they could not support their families and were forced to rely on soup kitchens for food. Some people "rode the rails," that is, they jumped onto empty boxcars and rode in them without paying for the ride, as they searched for work. Many people lived in "hobo jungles," encampments of jobless workers who congregated near the rail yards. Children who lived in the hobo jungles would try to sell pencils or apples on the streets to earn money.

F.D.R., as President Roosevelt was known, established government programs to create jobs for workers and to stimulate the economy. One of his government's programs, the Works Project Administration (WPA), provided construction jobs for workers who were unemployed and who could not otherwise find work. The WPA's building program included the construction of 116,000 buildings, 78,000 bridges, and 651,000 miles of roadways. The WPA's building program was also responsible for improvements to 800 airports. Other projects funded through the WPA were the Federal Art Project, the Federal Writers' Project, and the Federal Theatre Project. Many public buildings (especially post offices) were decorated with murals. The WPA gave dignity to workers who did not want to accept charity or handouts. They felt that they had made a contribution, from buildings to roads to art works to writing, in return for their government subsidies.

Roosevelt was President for much of Avi's childhood. He was the only president to serve more than two terms. His programs, including the WPA, helped lead the country out of the economic turmoil of the Great Depression. Avi's family supported his economic agenda, believing that the government should help workers regain their jobs. Roosevelt's leadership lasted beyond the Great Depression and into World War II.

World War II began in Europe before Avi was born. In 1936, Adolf Hitler's armies began to invade countries that bordered Germany. For the United States, suffering the end of the Depression, the war in Europe seemed very far away. Travel from New York to Europe, for instance, took a week on an ocean liner. Very few people flew across the Atlantic. In the days before the invention of the jet engine, the trip took eighteen hours and was very expensive.

European countries such as France and England, which had suffered enormous losses of life during World War I, were not anxious to go to war again. They did nothing to stop Hitler until he invaded Poland in 1939. Britain and France then declared war on Germany.

The United States, still feeling that the war would be limited to Europe, did not enter the conflict. Even when France was invaded in 1940, politicians called isolationists, who wanted to keep America free from alliances that would lead the nation to war, kept America neutral. The British suffered months of bombing raids in what would be called the Battle of Britain during the summer and fall of 1940. The Lend-Lease Act in 1941 provided American military equipment to foreign governments on extremely favorable terms. Yet the United States still did not join the British, declare war, or commit American troops to the conflict.

On December 7, 1941, just weeks before Avi's fourth birthday, emergency news broadcasts interrupted the regular radio programs. The special reports described an attack by Japanese aircraft against United States Navy ships and personnel. The predawn strike at Pearl Harbor, Hawaii, one of the Navy's largest bases in the Pacific, destroyed many ships and killed thousands of soldiers and sailors. The attack had severe consequences for the Japanese, for the United States, and for the rest of the world. By evening, the United States declared war on Japan and its partners. The United States joined the Allies, including France, Britain, and Russia, who opposed the Axis, comprised of Adolf Hitler's Nazi Germany, Italy, and Japan. Life in the United States, and for Avi's family, was to change dramatically during the war years.

WORLD WAR II

Mobilization for warfare began soon after the attack on Pearl Harbor. Fear grew that a bombing raid might be made on New York City. Civilian defense programs were created that instructed families how to ensure the city's safety. Blackouts were declared at night. People pulled heavy black curtains across their windows so that no trace of light could escape. Cars were kept off the streets, except for civil defense patrols that drove without their headlights. The defense patrols checked to see that no lights were visible and that citizens kept off the streets. The rationale was that without city lights to lead them to the city, enemy planes would not be able to find New York City and drop their bombs.

When Avi began kindergarten in 1942, he had to wear an identity tag to school every day. In the event of an attack, schools might have to be evacuated, and parents might be separated from their children. The identity tags would help make sure that parents would be able to find their own children. For Avi, blackouts and identity tags brought the war close to home and made it threatening. As it happened, no attacks were made on the continental United States.

Many of the fathers of Avi's friends were drafted or volunteered to serve in the armed forces. They went to train away from home and then went into action in North Africa, Sicily, Europe, and the Pacific. Many men were gone for months, sometimes even years. Avi's father was asked to serve in the Merchant Marine as a psychiatrist. Rather than seeing patients in his office inside the Wortis home, he dressed every morning in his Navy uniform and left to work at a facility in New York City. His patients were sailors who needed psychological treatment after suffering the traumas of the wartime attacks on their ships. The family was fortunate that Dr. Wortis was able to come home every night, unlike most people who served in the war.

In addition to Dr. Wortis's service in the Navy, the war meant a housing shortage in New York. Many people came to New York to help create material for the war effort. As the owners of a large house, the Wortis family had rooms they could rent to out to lodgers needing a place to live. One lodger was a medical student, who kept a skeleton in his room. This student became one of the characters in Avi's book about World War II, *"Who Was that Masked Man, Anyway?"* The book's title came from *The Lone Ranger*, one of the radio programs that Avi enjoyed. The Lone Ranger wore a mask and helped rescue people in the Old West. He was a popular character throughout the 1940s.

Besides the lack of housing, there were other shortages caused by war production. Food was rationed, which meant that a family was limited to a certain amount of specific products per person. Ration books were distributed to each family for meat, as well as sugar, butter, and coffee. People saved and recycled paper, tin cans, aluminum foil, and scrap metal. Even ladies' nylon stockings were in short supply, as factories that manufactured them were converted to create supplies for the war.

Avi's extended family remained close and saw each other frequently, despite the changes brought about by the war. Surrounded by books, storytellers, and lively intellectual debates, Avi's early environment was characterized by the love of words, fables, stories, and folk tales. His own enjoyment of learning surfaced early. By the age of five, Avi had taught himself to read. His ability to write, however, did not match his early reading skills. He suffered from symptoms of dyslexia, a learning disability characterized by problems in spelling, proofreading, proper use of capital letters, and writing legibly. As early as first grade in 1943, Avi's difficulties with writing became a source of insecurity and criticism.

The events of World War II formed the backdrop for much of Avi's early youth. On June 6, 1944, American and other allied troops went ashore in Normandy, France, beginning an all-out assault on northern France. It was the beginning of a sweep through Europe that would end in the defeat of Nazi Germany.

2

High School and Tutoring

CHILDHOOD IN THE 1940S

AVI'S FAMILY, LIKE many others in the United States, marked the progress of the war on a map. In early 1943, American soldiers fought in North Africa. Meanwhile, troops were being sent to England as the Allies prepared to cross the English Channel into France. On D-Day, June 6, 1944, American troops landed in Normandy and began the invasion of Europe.

On April 12, 1945, as Avi listened to a cowboy show, *Tom Mix*, on the radio, a reporter interrupted to give a news announcement. President Roosevelt had suffered a cerebral hemorrhage. Later that evening, over dinner, the family listened to a broadcast that gave the news about Roosevelt's death. Even though he was only seven, Avi knew that the President's death was a great loss for the country. Avi remembered a sense of sadness and grief for the only president he had known.[9] A few months later, in June 1945, Avi heard radio reports about Japan's surrender and the end of World War II.

With the end of the war, America entered a period of prosperity and economic growth. Soldiers returning to civilian life were eligible for many government benefits, from college tuition to inexpensive home loans. Wartime shortages of rubber and nylon ended, and families that had gotten used to rationing now had abundant gasoline, meat, and clothing.

In the 1940s, unlike today, twins were usually placed in the same classroom instead of being separated. Avi and his twin sister Emily were together for most of their elementary years at their local school, Public School 8. Emily, an excellent student, received rewards and praise for her schoolwork from their teachers and from their mother and father.

Avi, meanwhile, brought home papers covered with red marks and poor grades. He had difficulty with spelling and handwriting, and he spelled inconsistently. On one line, he would spell a word correctly. A few sentences later, he would spell it a different way. Avi's inability to proofread was a serious symptom of dyslexia. He was not able to catch his inconsistencies. Yet his teachers knew he was intelligent, articulate, and a good reader. Avi was often criticized as lazy or sloppy, when in fact he was trying his best.

"In a school environment, I was perceived as being sloppy and erratic, and not paying attention" [he wrote]. Despite constant criticism at school, Avi kept writing. . . . When papers came back covered in his teacher's red ink, he simply saved them, corrections and all. "I think there was so much criticism, I became immune to it. . . . I wasn't even paying attention to it. I liked what I wrote."[10]

The other children in the family, his older brother Henry and twin sister Emily, received more attention from their parents than Avi. Henry was brilliant at school and was regarded as a genius by their parents. Emily, in addition to being a good student, had a troubling heart murmur that required medical attention. Her heart did not pump as strongly as a normal heart should; she tired easily, and in general her health was delicate.

Dr. and Mrs. Wortis's anxiety over Emily's heart murmur caused them to shelter and protect her. They focused on her needs. Emily was often told to do her best, while Avi was told he just was not trying hard enough. Eventually, they decided to have a new type of medical treatment to correct Emily's heart murmur. Emily became one of the first children in the United States to have open-heart surgery.

Medicine in general was much less advanced than it is today. A disease called polio killed or paralyzed an average of 50,000 people, most of them children, every year. Today, the polio vaccine is commonly given in infancy, but in the 1940s, the vaccine had not yet been invented. Children who came down with polio might become paralyzed and unable to walk. Severe cases of polio could cause children to be unable to breathe on their own. They might spend the rest of their lives inside "iron lungs," huge machines that helped them breathe and stay alive. Other diseases like diphtheria, whooping cough, or measles that are commonly prevented by vaccines today killed many children in the 1940s.

Polio was feared more than other diseases, because it killed or disabled more children. To prevent exposure to polio, many families left the cities for summer vacations at the seashore. Not knowing exactly how the virus spread, families believed that the summer heat caused polio. The Wortis family went to a variety of places before buying a house on Shelter Island, east of New York City. Fathers stayed in the city to work and only came down to the shore on weekends.

Mothers did not often work outside the home. Women commonly were fired from their jobs when they married or as soon as they became pregnant. During World War II, many women had entered the work force to do jobs that had been vacated by men who joined the armed forces. When World War II ended, women were forced to give the jobs back to the men returning from the war.

A number of activities that are common for children today did not exist in the 1940s. Home computers and video games had not been invented. A family that wanted to go out for a quick meal would go to a soda fountain, a coffee shop, or a diner. There were only a few fast-food restaurants in all of New York City. Hamburger was usually ground at home from fresh meat bought at the butcher's shop. A different shop, the greengrocer, would supply vegetables. Milk was delivered to a family's back door. Horse-drawn milk wagons were common in many cities throughout the 1940s.

Did you know...

The Internet did not exist when Avi was a boy. To find information, a child had to go to the library and check out a book.

Many families, including Avi's, employed full-time servants. Most maids, cooks, and gardeners were African American. Racial integration was severely limited, and many professions excluded people of African descent. Competition in sports such as baseball was closed to African Americans, due to what was called "the color bar." African Americans could play in the minor leagues, a series of farm teams that provided players for the major leagues, or a segregated Negro league but people of color could not move up to the majors like their Caucasian teammates. Educational opportunities were also limited for African Americans. Few members of minorities could hope to go to college or enter professions such as medicine, law, or teaching.

There were many other differences between life today and life in the 1940s. For Avi, the most important difference lay in school life. Special education classes did not exist. Specialized training for teachers to work with students who had learning disabilities was extremely limited. Students were blamed for what were seen as their own shortcomings, rather than being taught strategies that would help them overcome their learning challenges.

For Avi, life during World War II and in the 1940s after the war was a mixed time of happiness and frustration. His learning disability limited his academic performance despite his best efforts. At home, his parents, especially his father, were distant. The company of books, and the love of reading, provided hours of companionship for Avi.

ELEMENTARY SCHOOL

Students attended Avi's elementary school, Public School 8 in Brooklyn, from kindergarten through eighth grade, then went directly from elementary school to high school. Most

Fridays during elementary school, Avi brought a spelling test home with his weekly schoolwork. Only a few of the words on the test would be spelled correctly. Sometimes letters were reversed or an upper case letter would appear in the middle of a word. Sometimes the words were spelled phonetically. Other times, the spelling did not appear to have any relationship to how the word sounded. When he tried to proofread his work, his eye simply did not catch the errors, so he was unable to correct them. These types of writing difficulties are all symptoms of dyslexia.

Today, students with dyslexia learn to use computers at an early age. They are able to use the spell checker to find the correct spelling of words. Severely dyslexic students can use voice recognition equipment to bypass the keyboard entirely and put their writing directly onto the computer screen in digital format. In Avi's childhood, none of these writing aids were available. Home computers and computers in classrooms were not common until the late 1980s, forty years after Avi was in school.

Just as important as computerized writing aids are teacher training and support for children with learning disabilities. During Avi's childhood, few teachers were trained to diagnose or recognize disabilities. Teaching strategies did not incorporate special needs curricula. Most teachers, when confronted with a bright and articulate child like Avi, believed that the child was lazy or inattentive if that child performed poorly on specific tasks.

Sharing a classroom with Emily, his twin sister, added to Avi's problems at school. Her work was outstanding, and her grades were always excellent. They compared his work to Emily's, always unfavorably, criticizing his schoolwork and lack of academic achievement. Often frustrated, Avi retreated into the world of books.

At the age of eight or nine, Avi and Henry moved from the room they shared with Emily on the third floor up to their own rooms on the fourth floor. Privacy meant more isolation for Avi, but it also meant a refuge, a place to enjoy reading, his favorite activity. After school, Avi played outside with the other boys in the neighborhood. Avi and his friends played stickball, a game with the rules of baseball, but with a motley assortment of gear, such as broomstick handles for bats, rubber balls instead of baseballs, and door mats or letterboxes as the bases. A favorite destination in the neighborhood was a carpenter's shop, where Avi was allowed to use scrap wood to build things. Avi would later use his carpentry skills as an adult, working odd jobs or building theater sets.

On most Saturday mornings, Avi, his brother and sister, and the other neighborhood children went to the movies. Instead of having theaters at shopping malls with multiple screens showing different movies on each screen, neighborhood theaters showed only one movie at a time on a single screen. Children's movies were often double-billed, with two films being screened back-to-back. Before the movie, a series of short subjects, such as cartoons or newsreels, were played. Without television, news events on film were shown only in movie houses. After the feature, an episode from a serial was played. Some favorites included the cowboy adventures of Hopalong Cassidy, or the science-fiction tales of Flash Gordon and his fight against the minions of Ming the Merciless in the twenty-fifth century. Because only one episode—which usually ended with Flash or Hopalong in dire peril—was shown, viewers returned every week to see how the hero escaped from death at the hands of his ruthless enemy. The movies themselves might include a feature-length cartoon by Walt Disney, such as

The years 1935 to 1945 were the golden age of the movie serial. An episode of a serial such as **Flash Gordon** *would accompany a feature movie and end with the hero (Flash Gordon, here with his archrival Ming the Merciless) in a perilous situation that would be resolved in the next installment. Like most children his age, Avi attended the movies on a weekly basis.*

Pinocchio or *Bambi*, a Tarzan melodrama, or a comedy with Bud Abbott and Lou Costello.

Just as important as trips to the movies were the weekly visits to the public library. Stocking up on reading material was serious business. After homework was finished, after radio shows were done, there would be nightly hours of browsing through books. Avi's favorite early books were animal stories, such as *The Wind in the Willows* by Kenneth Grahame. As he grew older, his favorites grew to include *Kidnapped* and *Treasure Island* by Robert Louis Stevenson.

He enjoyed reading magazines like *Popular Science* and *Popular Mechanics*. Sometimes he thought he would like to design airplanes when he grew up. He was particularly fascinated by jet engines.[11]

"*20,000 Leagues Under the Sea* had the most impact on me," wrote Avi. "I remember that book in particular because it was the first time I ever stayed up all night reading a book. The sinister nature of Captain Nemo fascinated me."[12]

Despite his love of reading, writing continued to be a problem. "Not performing up to his potential" was a frequent criticism made about Avi's schoolwork. Teachers did not understand how a child who read as much as Avi did, and who had a vivid imagination, could not produce paragraphs that were written correctly. Instead of looking for what he had to say, they looked only at the mechanics of his writing. His grades were average, unlike those of his brother and sister.

Summers at the shore became a blessed respite from school. In 1945, for $7,000, Joseph and Helen Wortis bought an abandoned farmhouse on Shelter Island, near the eastern tip of Long Island. It took hours in the car to get to the island, with the final minutes spent on a car-ferry between Long Island and Shelter Island.

At the old farmhouse, there was no indoor toilet, only an outhouse. Kerosene lamps provided light when the unreliable electricity failed. A wood-burning stove was used for cooking and provided warmth on chilly mornings. Water was pumped into the kitchen sink by a hand-pump. Although the farmhouse lacked the comforts of home, the Wortis children loved going to the shore. They could wade or swim at the many beaches, bays, and inlets that lined the island. They collected seashells, rode their bikes, and went fishing. They were allowed to roam freely, all day long, without constraints. Avi has used the island as a setting in several of his books, such as *A Place Called Ugly*, *Smuggler's Cove*, and *Captain Grey*.

By eighth grade, Avi decided that he did not want to be in the same class as his sister. He asked to be assigned to a teacher who specialized in science instruction, Mr. Malakowski. When he graduated from eighth grade in 1951, Mr. Malakowski's good teaching, and Avi's strong interest, had its effect. Avi won the science prize.

HIGH SCHOOL

After Public School 8, Avi briefly attended a large, academically challenging school, Stuyvesant High School, the same school his older brother Henry attended. Avi spent a miserable quarter at his new school. The change from having one teacher to having a different teacher for every subject, which is difficult for many children, was particularly hard for Avi. Stuyvesant was a huge school, with 5,000 boys enrolled that year. It was so crowded that the school held double shifts. Avi went to school from noon to 5 P.M. Unlike Henry, who was a brilliant student and thrived in the competitive, challenging environment at Stuyvesant, Avi received all Fs on his first report card.

Over Thanksgiving, without any warning, Avi's parents told him that he wasn't going back to Stuyvesant. Avi was so happy at changing schools that he rooted for the opposing team at a football game that weekend. Rather than forcing him to continue at a large, impersonal school, Dr. and Mrs. Wortis had enrolled Avi at Elizabeth Irwin High School.

Elizabeth Irwin High's educational philosophy reflected the progressive views of the school's founder and namesake. Elizabeth Irwin (1880–1942) was the co-author of a landmark book, *Fitting the School to the Child*, in which she argued for schools that focused on the needs of children and on a whole-child approach to learning. As the current Elizabeth Irwin High School website states,

> The curriculum is based on a belief that goes back to the original progressive educators, who recognized that the driving force behind authentic learning is a combination of children's natural curiosity, creativity, purposes, values, learning styles and the very human desire to make sense out of the world around them. We remain committed to the value of active learning that places students at the center of their education under the expert guidance of an extraordinary and dedicated faculty.[13]

Avi puzzled his teachers at Elizabeth Irwin, as he had puzzled many other teachers in the past. He loved school, and he loved to read. He seemed to be a bright, intelligent, articulate boy, but his written work was full of mistakes. He spelled words different ways every time he used them. His handwriting was cramped and nearly impossible to read. Every paper that he turned in was returned to him covered with red marks. By his second year, his academic performance was so poor that he was in danger of failing to graduate. Fortunately, he met and began to work with his tutor, Ella Ratner. With hard work and perseverance, Avi began to do better in school.

Avi went to college at the University of Wisconsin in Madison, seen here, and graduated with a degree in history and theater in 1959. He completed the coursework for his Masters of Arts degree in drama in 1960, after which he moved across the country to try his hand at playwriting in San Francisco.

3

College and Theater

GRADUATION DAY

IN JUNE 1955, Avi walked across the stage of the auditorium at Elizabeth Irwin High School. He shook hands with the principal. The principal handed Avi his high school diploma. Avi returned quietly to his place with the other graduates. Most of them had expected to finish high school. In fact, they had taken graduation for granted. Few of the other students at Elizabeth Irwin had ever doubted that they would walk across the school stage and receive their high school diplomas.

Unlike his fellow students, Avi's graduation from high school had been in jeopardy in his sophomore year. After a summer of daily work with Ella Ratner, Avi's gifted tutor, Avi's grades improved, and he was able to complete high school. For Avi, high school graduation had required a high level of effort, concentration, and perseverance.

A high school diploma was not only an end in itself for Avi, it was also a key step to his future. If he had not completed high school, Avi would not have been able to continue his education. Colleges or universities would not have accepted him as a student. Many professions would have been barred to him. Most importantly, Avi would have found it very difficult to pursue his career goal. By March 1955, the year he graduated from high school, Avi had decided that he wanted to be a writer. He wrote in his diary, "I can't wait any more. I'm going to become a playwright." [14]

COLLEGE DAYS

After high school, Avi enrolled in Antioch College in Yellow Springs, Ohio. The college had a nontraditional curriculum that afforded students a liberal, experimental education, but it proved to be too unstructured for Avi. He transferred to the University of Wisconsin in Madison, where he majored in history and theater.

In noting people's reactions to his descriptions of his majors, Avi underlined an important point about word choice. "When I was an undergraduate at the University of Wisconsin in the 1950s," Avi wrote, "I had two major fields of study, history and theater. Nowadays, young people evaluate one another by the way they dress or by what music their ears are plugged into. In my day—since we were outwardly vastly more conformist and couldn't tell books or people by their covers—you inquired of a person you had just met, 'What are you majoring in?' I, with two majors, had a choice of responses. I could say 'History.' I could say 'Theater.' In either case I would be telling the truth. If I wished not to continue the social contact, I would say 'History.' That drove the person away. If I wanted to impress the person, I would say 'Theater,' which seemed to make me a very interesting person indeed. That label fairly glittered."[15]

Although he still struggled with spelling, Avi wrote constantly. Playwriting courses gave him structure and focus for his writing. "That's where I started to write seriously," he wrote. "The first playwriting instructor that I had would say, 'This is the way you do it.' You didn't have much choice in it; you had to do it in a very specific way. He even had charts for you to fill out. And I think I learned how to organize a story. . . . I think, although I'm not sure of this, that [the playwriting structure from college] that is still the structure I use when I write."[16]

He submitted a play to the college playwriting contest in his senior year. Unfortunately, his learning disability continued to be a problem. One of the judges in the contest thought Avi was an English language learner. "This person obviously is not an English-speaking person," the judge wrote, "but he is making great strides in learning the language and should be encouraged."[17]

Nevertheless, Avi persisted in his studies and in playwriting. In 1959, he earned his college degree, a Bachelor of Arts in history and theater. He remained at the University of Wisconsin for another year after graduation to study playwriting. He completed the coursework for his Master of Arts degree in drama, although due to the timing of the coursework and the graduation ceremony the degree itself was not awarded until commencement in 1962.

At the end of his year of graduate studies, Avi submitted another play to the writing contest, and this time he won. His play, *A Little Rebellion*, a comedy about the American Revolution, was published in two magazines. The university staged a production of it. With his first successful play behind him, Avi decided to leave the university and move across the country.

SAN FRANCISCO AND NEW YORK

Avi moved to San Francisco in 1960 to be the resident playwright at the World Theater. San Francisco was the home to the Beat Generation poets like Jack Kerouac, Allen Ginsberg, and Lawrence Ferlinghetti. San Francisco's liberal and literary legacy dated back to 1849, when Mark Twain visited and described the boomtown that had grown up after the Gold Rush brought an immigration of fortune hunters. Other authors who had lived and worked for a time in San Francisco included Robert Louis Stevenson, who wrote about the mining camps along the Silverado Trail north of San Francisco. Jack London, whose book *The Call of the Wild* was used as an example of books children were forced to read in school in Avi's book *Nothing but the Truth*, was born across the bay from San Francisco, in the city of Oakland.

As resident playwright, Avi did not receive any salary for his work. He was allowed to sleep in the back of the theater. By day, he printed signs in a department store to earn money. The goal of any playwright is to see his work performed on stage, but the financial investment in mounting a performance can be large. Generally, a playwright seeks backers to provide money for renting the theater space and paying the actors,

Did you know...

New York City's Lincoln Center for the Performing Arts, where Avi worked, is the world's largest performing arts complex.

stagehands, costume designers, ticket vendors, and publicity team. Before people will invest in a play, they must be convinced that they are not going to lose their money and that the play has a reasonable chance to be popular with the public.

Avi spent a year in San Francisco, but none of his plays were produced. Backers had been unwilling to invest their money in any of his works. In 1961, he returned to New York to be closer to the heart of American theater, the "Great White Way," as Broadway was called. He had a written a trunkful of plays, and he hoped to see them on the stage.

In New York, since Avi was not the resident playwright at a theater, he had to find a way to support himself. To keep his schedule free for writing, he worked part-time in a restaurant. He painted signs (although some of them were misspelled) and used the skills he had learned as a boy to do carpentry work. He worked as a drama coach, teaching children how to act.

The 1960s was a decade of change, both for the country and for Avi. John F. Kennedy won the presidency in 1960, but he was assassinated before the end of his first term in office. He was succeeded in office by Lyndon Baines Johnson, who increased America's involvement in Vietnam. The war became increasingly unpopular as many Americans questioned the administration's belief in the "domino theory," which held that if one nation fell to Communism, the other surrounding nations would fall, just like a line of dominos will fall if the first one is knocked over. Many others questioned America's commitment to the war, believing that putting troops on the ground on foreign turf without an all-out invasion caused soldiers' lives to be wasted. Student demonstrations and sometimes-violent protests called for an end to the war.

Racial integration was another area of change. Calls had begun in the 1950s for integration throughout American society. Segregated districts, where African-American and white children did not attend the same schools, were challenged and found to be unconstitutional in the 1954 landmark case, *Brown* v. *Board of Education*. The color bar in baseball had fallen in 1948, when Jackie Robinson signed with Avi's home team, the Brooklyn Dodgers, and became the first African-American player in the major leagues. Despite these gains, discrimination remained common throughout America. President Johnson signed the Civil Rights Act in 1964. The Act outlawed discrimination in voter registration requirements and in hotels, motels, restaurants, and theaters; encouraged the desegregation of public schools; authorized the withdrawal of federal funds from programs that practiced discrimination; and outlawed discrimination in employment.[18] Dr. Martin Luther King, Jr., advocated peaceful resistance to segregation and discrimination, but he in turn was assassinated on April 4, 1968.

During the 1960s, women began to demand equality in the workplace. After the end of World War II, women, who had done everything from driving trucks to building ships to welding, were forced to give up their jobs when the men returned from the war. Their daughters, in the 1960s, demanded not only equality in opportunities for jobs, but also equal pay for equal work.

New kinds of music and new forms of entertainment became popular in the 1960s. Television—only three national channels in black and white—broadcast the news, dramas, comedies, and other programming. Musicians, such as the Beatles, Elvis Presley, and Stevie Wonder brought different rhythms, instruments, beats, and sounds to the music scene.

For Avi, New York was culturally rich but financially less than rewarding. He wrote constantly, but his plays did not receive the recognition of being produced. Yet this fertile period, where Avi supported himself with odd jobs in order to have time to write, was reflected in Avi's later works. He wrote, "My early writing as a playwright continues to influence the way I conceptualize a story and its structure. . . . My understanding of the way a plot moves forward is derived from my sense and experiences in the theater."[19] Avi persisted, despite the lack of recognition for his plays, because, as one interviewer has noted, "he simply loves to write."[20]

Avi's parents continued to be distant and did not recognize his achievements. For Christmas, in his first year of college, Avi wrote a long poem that he gave to his mother. She never mentioned reading it until he asked her, years later, what she had thought of the poem. She told him that there were part of it that were good and she believed that he had plagiarized those parts. She felt that the parts that were not as well written were the ones he had written himself.[21]

Being a drama coach was one of the most rewarding of Avi's part-time jobs. Not only did he maintain his connection with the theater when he worked with budding actors, he found personal rewards as well. He gave coaching sessions at the Young Men's Hebrew Association (a nonprofit cultural center with goals similar to those of the Young Men's Christian Association). One day, Avi met a dance teacher named Joan Gainer. They began dating and soon planned to marry. Instead of patching together a living from occasional part-time jobs, Avi looked for regular employment.

THE NEW YORK PUBLIC LIBRARY

One day as he was trying to find a job, Avi visited the New York Public Library. He learned that the theater department needed a clerk. It was an excellent opportunity for a young man who loved the theater and who loved books. Avi applied for and gained the position.

The New York Public Library, where Avi began a career as clerk in 1962. After getting a degree in library science, Avi got a job at the New York Public Library for the Performing Arts, at Lincoln Center. The position was the beginning of a twenty-five year career as a librarian.

Working at the library gave Avi much-needed financial stability. He no longer worked at a variety of part-time jobs to support himself. He continued to write during most of his spare time. Although he now held a full-time job, he still wrote every day, working on plays and trying to find backers for them.

Soon after he began to work at the library, Avi learned that the performing arts collection would be moved to Lincoln Center as soon as the Center was completed. Lincoln Center would be the most advanced, technically sophisticated performing arts center in the country. When the library moved, only highly qualified workers would be employed. Avi needed an advanced degree in order to be sure that he would be able to keep his job after the move to Lincoln Center.

Avi decided to enroll at Columbia University, studying library science at night while working during the day. He found a backer for one of his plays and began to prepare for the play to be produced. The financial deal fell through, and the play never aired on the New York stage. However, there was one good result from the experience. Avi's backer encouraged him to get a literary agent, a person who would represent him to publishers and who would try to sell his works. Having a literary agent was one thing that separated professional writers from people who wrote as a hobby or who did not consider it as their profession. Acceptance by a literary agent meant that Avi was now a recognized professional, even though none of his works had been sold yet.

A friend encouraged Avi to try writing novels instead of plays, since novels were much more likely to be sold and published than plays were likely to be performed. Avi wrote several novels, and his agent showed them to editors at publishing houses. Despite his lack of publishing success, Avi continued in his commitment to writing. Working during the day and going to school at night, Avi nevertheless completed nearly 800 pages of a novel. He still wanted to communicate his ideas, to have readers think about the questions he posed in his stories. The difficulty lay in getting his works into the hands of the reading public.

In the meantime, Avi's romance with Joan blossomed. On November 1, 1963, Joan Gainer and Avi were married at a Unitarian church in New York. It was a private ceremony, without guests or even the bride and groom's parents. Afterwards, Avi and Joan went to the home of Avi's parents to tell them the news.

Avi completed his master's degree in library science from Columbia in 1964. He worked at the Lincoln Center library, in the performing arts collection. The position was the beginning of a twenty-five year career as a librarian.

In 1968, Avi arranged a job exchange with an English librarian and spent a year living and working in London, England. His second son, Kevin, was born in England, and Avi spent many hours spinning tales for his two sons as well as reading other writers' books to them. Some of these tales would become the basis of Avi's first book, Things That Sometimes Happen, which was published not long after the family returned from England.

4

Father, Librarian, Teacher, and Writer

A NEW ADDITION TO THE FAMILY

AVI AND JOAN'S son Shaun was born in 1966. Although he had a job and a family, Avi still spent most of his spare time writing. With Shaun, Avi found a new outlet for his storytelling skills. He played a game with Shaun, called "Tell me a story."

"My oldest would tell me what the story should be about— he would invent stuff, a story about a glass of water and so forth. It became a game, and here I had a writing background so I was telling some fairly sophisticated stories."[22]

Shaun gave Avi the story ideas—a black crayon, a subway ride, a kite, or an ice cream cone—and Avi spun tales around the prototypical central characters. These tales would later become the basis of Avi's first published book, *Things That Sometimes Happen.*

Avi tried other creative outlets as well. He enjoyed drawing and thought he might use his skills professionally. He designed and illustrated greeting cards. A friend who received one encouraged him to try publishing the cards. Eager for a way to supplement his librarian's salary, Avi attempted to sell his ideas for the greeting cards. Although he did not make any sales, his illustrations captured the imagination of a friend who wrote children's books. She liked his drawings so much that she asked him to illustrate her next work.

Avi agreed, and the friend sent the text she had written and Avi's illustrations to an editor at a publishing company. The editor did not buy the work, but she liked Avi's drawings. She asked Avi if he would be interested in illustrating other books. He considered himself to be a writer and told her so. The editor suggested that he both write and illustrate a children's book. The combination of his story and his drawings, the editor believed, might be publishable as a children's book.

Avi worked on a tight deadline: in two weeks, he and his family were due to leave for England. That year, 1968, Avi had arranged a job exchange with an English librarian. For a year, Avi planned to work at a library in England, while the English librarian would work at Avi's job in New York. To write the book, Avi wrote, "I took a week off of work. Some neighbors were gone and I used their apartment. I put down all the stories that I had told my son and drew the pictures, all within one week."[23]

In writing about the stories in *Things That Sometimes Happen*, critics Susan Bloom and Cathryn Mercier commented, "The individual stories run anywhere from a half-page to four pages in length. They center on an ordinary event, although a dreamlike quality often transforms that ordinary occurrence into an extraordinary one. For example, a little boy walking in the park soon finds himself in the jungle, where he discovers an enormous green mushroom. The title story introduces the conjunction of the child's here-and-now and the fantastical world of her imagination . . . In the book's final piece, entitled 'A Story about a Story,' Avi constructs an eloquent description of story as having 'lots of interesting things to say, even funny things. It went on, on, with all sorts of things happening' requiring an ending."[24]

Avi turned in the manuscript and illustrations before he, Joan, and Shaun left for England. Avi's second son, Kevin, was born while the family lived in England. They enjoyed their foreign stay, seeing the sights of London and other British cities. A trip to Spain began in historic Plymouth, where the Pilgrims departed England for America aboard the *Mayflower*. Avi and his family embarked on a car ferry from Plymouth and sailed first across the English Channel and then across part of the Atlantic Ocean to the north coast of Spain. With baby Kevin riding in a pack on Avi's back and smiling at other vacationers, they made friends easily.

Did you know...

The steps that the Pilgrims walked down to board the *Mayflower* still exist in Plymouth. Avi visited them when living in England.

Even before he could speak, Kevin began listening to Avi's stories. With two children, Avi found an attentive audience. In addition to spinning tales for them and reading his own works to them, Avi read extensively from other writers' books. He learned, as they either listened closely or yawned in boredom, what children enjoyed as read-aloud books. Later, he learned what they liked to read to themselves. They gave him an early education in children's writing. He got as much, or more, out of reading aloud as they did. "My children gave me my profession," wrote Avi.[25]

After their year in England, they returned to the United States in 1969. Avi found that supporting a family of four on the New York Public Library's salary was difficult. He found a better-paying position at Trenton State College (now called The College of New Jersey) in New Jersey. The family moved to Trenton in 1970.

TRENTON STATE COLLEGE

The move proved an excellent choice for Avi. In addition to his primary job, as a librarian, he occasionally taught classes in children's literature. He believed that reading fosters writing, and he started a collection of children's books. He picked up and bought books wherever he found them—at garage sales, book fairs, and used bookstores—to add to his collection. He bought many books on history, reflecting his life-long interest in the past. Avi's collection grew, until it numbered 3,000 volumes.

At Trenton State College, Avi worked as a reference librarian. A critic wrote about Avi's career as a librarian, "One element stands as a key to reading Avi—recognition of the sheer quantity of knowledge and insight he commands about literature for children and young adults. He is trained as a librarian, practices as a teacher of children's and young adult literature for children and adults, [and] writes critical and reflective essays as well as novels"[26]

Avi also wrote about his views, as a historian, of the development of children's literature in the United States. In doing so, Avi "challenges the traditional understanding of children's literature as derived from a British tradition. Avi argues convincingly that a distinctly American view of childhood—as a unique developmental period with a literature of subversion—forced a break from the British tradition of literature as a training ground for adulthood."[27]

Children, in Avi's view, were not blank pages to be written on by adults. Rather, he saw childhood as a time when a child developed a personal identity, unique to the child and inspired by the child's own needs and abilities. In describing the literature of subversion, Avi meant the literature that encouraged children to resist the indoctrination that adults tried to force on them or that encouraged children to create their own stories, their own histories, and by extension, their own systems of beliefs and their own personalities.

Working at Trenton State College gave Avi an opportunity to meet teachers-in-training who were studying for their teaching credentials. He also met many professors of education, who taught the classes that aspiring teachers were required to take. His point of view about elementary teaching was different from that of most education professors. He wrote, "For many years I worked as a librarian in a state college. The education professors labored mightily to achieve curriculum enhancements in the teacher education program. They were thrilled when they pushed and got their top priority: two required courses on the *method* of teaching reading. Do you know how many required courses in literature would-be elementary teachers were required to take?

One. In other words, methodology was more important than content. To me this was like offering courses in lifesaving techniques to prospective swimming instructors but neglecting to teach the art of swimming."[28]

Avi believed that elementary teachers needed to learn about literature for children. Many teachers entered the profession because they liked to read children's books, but few had taken classes that gave a systematic, organized, or critical approach to children's literature. Avi created courses that examined critical appraisals of a writer's work and that compared and contrasted his or her books with those of other writers.

Avi's book, *Things That Sometimes Happen*, based on the stories he had told to Shaun, had been rejected by the editor who had originally asked Avi to write and illustrate it. Avi's agent believed that the work had potential and kept sending it out to other editors. Avi wrote, ". . . seven publishers down the road, Doubleday accepted it."[29]

FIRST BOOK

Avi's first book, *Things That Sometimes Happen*, was published in 1970. Interestingly enough, the text was accepted but not the illustrations. This outcome was an ironic one, since Avi's illustrations for a friend's book had originally brought him into the field of children's literature. Fifteen years after he had declared that he wanted to be a writer, Avi's work had broken into print.

Publication of the book changed Avi's writing goals immediately. He abandoned writing for adults to concentrate all his efforts on children's books. With his first books, he tended to write at the current reading level of his own sons, picture books when they were little and easy chapter books when they learned to read independently.

Before the publication of *Things That Sometimes Happen*, Avi's agent asked him what name he wanted on the book's cover. "That's an odd question to ask," wrote Avi. "It was never an issue, but I thought about it and I said, 'Oh well, just put Avi down,' and that was the decision. Just like that."[30]

Avi's second book, *Snail Tail*, was published in 1972. It is a chapter book about the adventures of two creatures, a circular tale that ends where it began. Unlike *Things That Sometimes Happen*, which is a book about different creatures and personified ideas, *Snail Tale* has two main characters: Avon the snail and his friend Edward the ant. They leave home, have adventures, and return home again. When friends ask about their most exciting experience, Avon recounts an episode that never really happened. Critic Margery Fisher wrote, "[*Snail Tail*] is a light-hearted satire on the way a writer manipulates reality. Avon's reverential belief in the infallibility of traditional literature is seen to be relevant. . . . Hearing a sound of woe in the distance, he announces, 'I think we should stop. . . . That's what they do in books.'"[31] *Snail Tail* was rewritten and published with a new title, *The End of the Beginning*, in 2004.

Snail Tale is, in many ways, a book about storytelling. At the beginning of the book, Avon is shown as reading constantly. Avi, when asked how he would teach children to write, responded, "I think it's very simple. The most difficult thing about writing is reading. And the most important thing that you can do to become a writer is read. . . . If you read a lot, you begin to shape your thinking process as a storytelling mechanism."[32]

For his first few years as a published author, Avi concentrated on writing books that were geared to his sons' reading levels. However, they soon outpaced him and were reading books that were at a more advanced reading level than the books Avi was writing. He wrote, "At a certain point they kept growing and I didn't. I hit a fallow period, and then I wrote *No More Magic.* Suddenly I felt 'This is right! I'm writing novels and I love it.' From then on I was committed to writing novels."[33]

In 1976, the family moved from New Jersey to New Hope, Pennsylvania. The family, with two growing boys and Avi's growing book collection, needed a larger house. Joan, formerly a dancer, had become a weaver. She needed room for a studio to hold her loom, yarns, and other materials.

A WRITER'S LIFE

As more of his books were published, Avi began to make school visits. He enjoyed meeting his readers face to face. With his friend and fellow-writer Betty Miles, he wrote an article about school visits. In it, they wrote, "We are authors who like to talk with our readers. . . . The goal of the visit, overall, is to make each child feel personally connected to the author, and by extension, more enthusiastic about books and more knowledgeable about books and writing. . . . Above all, the visit is for the students."[34]

Avi's visits usually included a chance to meet separately with the special education classes. Students in these classes might share his learning disability or might have similar ones. "They come in slowly, waiting for yet another pep talk, more instructions. Eyes cast down, they won't even look at me. Their anger glows: I don't say a thing. I lay out pages of my copy-edited manuscripts, which are covered with red marks. 'Look here,' I say, 'see that spelling mistake. Now here, a run-on sentence. There, another spelling mistake. Looks like I forgot to put a capital letter here. Oops! Letter reversal.' Their eyes lift. They are listening.

And I am among friends."[35] Avi's examples show the children that they can overcome their disabilities just as he had overcome dyslexia.

Avi's job as a librarian gave him the flexibility to make room in his schedule for school visits. He could work long hours for a few days and then take a morning or a day off to spend in the classroom with his readers. He stayed at Trenton State for seventeen years. In addition to his job in the library and his busy schedule of school visits, he taught courses at several colleges on children's literature. One of his innovations was looking at the whole body of writers' works, from their first books to their most recent publications. This methodology differed from the traditional way that literature was generally taught, where only a few books of a particular author would be studied. The method worked, as Avi reported that fellow authors called and asked to be studied ". . . in this thorough and serious manner. Indeed, at least one author rejoiced in learning something new about herself as expressed in her writing from this careful, thoughtful group of readers."[36]

Children's literature in the 1970s and early 1980s was not nearly as rich or rewarding financially for authors as it is in the post-Harry Potter era. Before J.K. Rowling's saga of Harry Potter and his adventures, there had never been a blockbuster children's book. Children's books were not counted in the sales figures that went into the bestsellers' lists. Reviews for children's books were limited, for the most part, to the pages of specialized publications for teachers and librarians. Few reviews of books for children were printed in the newspapers, where many readers learn about new and upcoming books. Avi described his opinions about why children's books were not treated seriously in an article for the *Horn Book*, one of the few magazines devoted entirely to children's literature: "Make no mistake about it: *children's literature is a woman's world.*"

> What I want to suggest to you is that children's literature is ill-recognized, ill-supported, considered uninteresting *because* it is a world created in large measure by women for a readership [of librarians and teachers] which in large measure is female. Furthermore, I believe those in children's literature are treated with a large measure of social contempt because our focus is children. . . . Those values which we culturally ascribe to women in stereotypical fashion are values associated with nurturing, sharing, nonviolence, cooperation, the ability to love; by extension they are connected to children's literature. . . . In truth it [children's literature] is treated badly because . . . [it] is critical of the adult world in which it exists.[37]

Avi's comments reflected the feminist recognition, which had begun in the 1970s, that women's traditional roles were not given the same value as those of men. Nurses, for example, who had advanced training and who could save lives, might make less money than a gardener or a janitor. Salaries for teachers and librarians were much less than those of mechanics or construction workers, despite the fact that teachers and librarians generally had higher levels of education and training than mechanics or construction workers. Many times, women were paid less than men for the same jobs. With the women's movement in the 1970s and 1980 came the recognition that equal pay should be awarded for equal work. Women began to demand access to jobs that had not traditionally been seen as suited for women, such as firefighter, scientist, computer systems analyst, and many others.

Mothers in all kinds of careers began to look for books that featured strong girls in active roles for both their sons and their daughters. They wanted their sons to read about girls and learn to respect them as much as they wanted their daughters to read about girls as the protagonists in books. Books were published showing children of different races going to school together and becoming friends. For writers, the social changes of feminism and racial integration meant that imagination and creativity could incorporate a much wider range of characters than ever.

The nineteenth-century author and poet Edgar Allan Poe was the inspiration for Avi's book The Man Who Was Poe. *The real Edgar Allan Poe virtually created the detective story and perfected the psychological thriller. He is the main character in this novel, in which Avi combines mystery with historical fiction.*

5

Full-time Writer

HISTORICAL NOVELS

AT TRENTON STATE College, Avi wrote his first historical novel, *Captain Grey*, which was published in 1977. He wrote about historical fiction,

History is never simple, finite, without contradiction, or even perfectly knowable. It is never completely objective. It is constantly changing. Those who write historical fiction are equally products of history. But the writer of historical fiction has a different task than the historian. Historical fiction uses the past so as to understand the present. . . . For example, let's say I write about a time in which girls were forbidden to do XYZ. That may be historically correct, but to simply retell that tale to today's girls is to say it's still not right for girls to do XYZ. I do not wish to do that. It is my desire to use the past to write about today.[38]

Yet while he might have shown people in unconventional roles, Avi's attention to historical authenticity was strong. He researched the settings and historical periods of his books with close attention to details about customs, local information, and patterns of speech. For *Beyond the Western Sea*, he paraphrased actual speeches that had been given at the time, and read rulebooks for workers. He consulted the first edition of *Roget's Thesaurus*, published in 1850.[39] For the award-winning book, *Crispin: The Cross of Lead*, he looked at a map of London in the 14th century and read poetry written at the time.[40]

For another book, *Don't You Know There's A War On?* Avi researched World War II, even though he had lived through it. He read *The New York Times* and learned details of the war that he had not realized at the time. Reading the newspaper also jogged his memory about coupon books, ration cards, and life in World War II. He also learned details that he had been unaware of as a child, such as the fact that the newspaper reported vividly on the battles, violence, and deaths due to the war.[41]

Many of Avi's books, in addition to showing strong girl characters, show parents who are distant and who do not communicate well with their children. Avi's own relationship with his parents continued to be distant and reflected their lack of understanding of his devotion to writing. Once, when he told his mother that he was publishing novels in addition to being a librarian, she said, "It's good to have a second string to your bow." She meant that writing was a good backup, or second career, in case Avi ever lost his job as a librarian. For Avi, writing was his vocation, while being a librarian was his backup "second string" career. Avi commented, "She got it completely backwards."[42]

LIFE CHANGES

Avi's background in theater and in playwriting helped him write compelling children's books.

> I try to write about complex issues—young people in an adult world—full of irony and contradiction, in a narrative style that relies heavily on suspense with a texture rich in emotion and imagery. I take a great deal of satisfaction in using popular forms—the adventure, the mystery, the thriller —so as to hold my reader with the sheer pleasure of a good story. At the same time, I try to resolve my books with an ambiguity that compels engagement. In short, I want my reader to feel, to think, sometimes to laugh. But most of all, I want them to enjoy a good read.[43]

Having been a playwright, Avi used dialogue extensively in his books. In fact, one of his editors made a suggestion

Did you know...

Avi's books have been translated into Korean, German, Italian, Thai, Portuguese, Italian, Japanese, Arabic, German, Spanish, French, Chinese, Danish, Greek, Dutch, Norwegian, and Austrian.

about dialogue. Avi and the editor, Richard Jackson, were watching an old movie in a theater in California. Jackson said, "Some day I'd like to see you write a book with just dialogue. I'll give you a few 'he said' and 'she saids'."[44]

The idea bore fruit, and Avi wrote *"Who Was that Masked Man, Anyway?"* a novel that consists completely of dialogue. There are no descriptions and, in fact, no "he saids" or "she saids." The reader is not told who is talking and what actions the characters are taking. Reading *"Who Was that Masked Man, Anyway?"* or hearing it read aloud is like experiencing one of the 1940s radio plays that the novel was based on. In the book, Avi used the scripts for some of his favorite radio plays, including *The Lone Ranger*, the masked man that the title refers to. Every *Lone Ranger* show included the tag line, "Who was that masked man, anyway?"

Avi wrote many novels at Trenton State, including the novel, *The Fighting Ground*, a book about the American Revolution that won the Scott O'Dell Award for Historical Fiction, and the comedic novel *S.O.R. Losers*, a book that shows an unenthusiastic, unathletic group of boys forced to play soccer.

Working long hours, writing in most of his spare time, traveling to visit schools, and engaging in his other writing-related activities such as teaching, took time away from his family and from his wife. After realizing that they had drifted apart, Avi and Joan divorced in 1982. Shaun went to college, and Avi lived near Joan and Kevin while Kevin finished high school.

After his divorce, Avi's sister Emily introduced him to one of her old college friends, Coppélia Kahn, a college professor. Avi and Coppélia were married a year later. Coppélia taught at Wesleyan College in Connecticut, so

Avi applied for a job as a librarian nearby. After about four years, he found one. But before he could start his new job, Coppélia was offered a position at Brown University in Providence, Rhode Island. Avi could have looked for another position as a librarian, but he decided instead to take a dramatic and courageous step. With both Kevin and Shaun in college, he decided not to find a job as a librarian. In 1987, Avi decided to become a full-time writer.

PROVIDENCE

Avi and Coppélia moved into a house in Providence, Rhode Island, that dated back to the 1830s. With his avid interest in history, Avi wondered about the house's past, its former owners, and what it would have been like to live there sometime early in the house's lifetime. The result of his research was the book *Something Upstairs*, which was published in 1988, the year after he moved to Providence. The story concerns twelve-year-old Kenny, a boy living in contemporary times who moved into a house similar to Avi's. Kenny saw the ghost of a young slave boy named Caleb. Kenny traveled back in time to help free Caleb's ghost.

Avi combined historical details about life in the 1800s with a strong theme concerning racism. He wrote, ". . . as far as our nation is concerned, issues of race and racism are paramount. No other problem is as fundamental to our past, our present, our future."[45]

Avi's family background, with its discussions of liberal topics and belief in equality for all persons regardless of gender or race, showed clearly in his work. In addition, Avi returned to the theme of story and storytelling. Kenny's story is written as if he had told it to Avi. By self-consciously calling attention to himself as the narrator who tells

Kenny's story, Avi gave the book "a dimension of eerie reality."[46] The reality that Avi evoked in *Something Upstairs* prompted the Providence Preservation Society to include Avi and Coppélia's house in its historical tours of the city.

In the years after his move to Providence and to full-time writing, Avi wrote a novel, sometimes two or three, every year. In 1989, he published *The Man Who Was Poe*, another historical novel that featured historically accurate details combined with a subtext about storytelling. The writer Edgar Allan Poe appears as a character in *The Man Who Was Poe*. Avi has Poe take the name of one of Poe's own characters, Auguste Dupin from *The Murders in the Rue Morgue* and other Parisian mysteries, in order to help a young boy, Edmund, find his missing twin sister and aunt. When Poe masquerades as a detective, he takes on the characteristics of his own fictional creation and is able to solve the mystery and locate Edmund's relatives.

Avi consciously wove levels of fiction and reality into the book, creating a tapestry of questions for his readers to answer. He believed that there was more than a single interpretation of his story. He further believed that the author might not be in control of the story, at many levels. Concerning the interactions of authors and readers, Avi wrote, "never fully trust the author, never fully trust my characters, never fully trust my story, not even my words. Above all, when you finish the story and come to a conclusion that you know what it means, it's crucial never to assume that *I* know what it means….Good *writing*, I think, comes about when the writer's conscious mastery of technique allows his or her unconscious to be revealed."[47]

Avi trusted his readers to make their own choices about the meanings of his stories. He wrote,

"Reading truly engages people's minds in a way no other art form does. You have to be part of what you read. You can't be passive."

Some adults find that interactive quality threatening.

"There are a lot of people who don't like kids in this country," he says. "They get scared when kids become too independent, and it's a legitimate fear. Because reading is very private, no one can tell what a child is thinking when they read. No one can control what they are thinking. That's why some people are afraid of books. For them, it's about authority. For them, it's about control."[48]

CHARLOTTE DOYLE

For his next book, *The True Confessions of Charlotte Doyle*, published in 1990, Avi received a Newbery Honor and a Boston Globe-Horn Book Award. *The True Confessions of Charlotte Doyle* is a historical novel, as well as a coming-of-age novel about the choices made by a young girl. Written from the first-person point of view, the novel is the story of Charlotte Doyle's journey from England to America on board the *Seahawk* in 1832. During the course of the Atlantic crossing, Charlotte must make choices that have a dramatic impact on her life, and on the lives of the *Seahawk's* crew. She ultimately makes, ". . . [the] daring choice of her own identity." Instead of staying in her parent's home, where she was forced to adopt the stifling class and gender restrictions she had rebelled against, Charlotte chooses to run away to the place where she had known true freedom. She runs away to rejoin the ship's crew.[49]

Charlotte's choice would seem, in an era of positive role models for girls and of independent thought for women, to be an uplifting, positive choice. Not always so, as Avi reported in his acceptance speech for the *Boston Globe-Horn Book* Award. A producer wanted to make a movie out of the book. She discussed the project with Avi, telling him that only one part of the book needed to be changed.

> . . . she confessed an absolute passion for this book . . . which considering the profession of the person talking—I took as an ominous warning. Still, bright money was being dangled before my bleary writer's eyes, so I listened. . . . As she talked, I tried to guess what changes she would make. Did they perhaps, wish to tone down the depictions of racism in the book? Or could it be that they felt compelled to soften the moments of brutality that evoked life on the old sailing ships? Might it be that they wished to modify the vicious cruelty of . . . Captain Jaggery?
>
> "No," she said, ending the suspense, "we'll have to change the ending."
>
> "The ending?" I said, truly surprised. "Why?"
>
> "Television can't show that."
>
> "By that," I wondered aloud, "do you mean Charlotte's choice of freedom?"
>
> "Exactly. It's felt it would encourage too many runaways."
>
> It was one of those rare moments when I was truly speechless. Finally, I said, "Well, what do you have in mind?"
>
> "Couldn't," she asked, "couldn't the girl stay home and reform her father?"
>
> "Oh," I said, recovering, "sort of die in childbirth to save the pig?"
>
> "Oh, good idea!" she cried.
>
> And I told her, "Sorry, you've got the wrong Charlotte."[50]

Wittily evoking the book *Charlotte's Web*, by E.B. White, Avi demonstrated that the producer had failed to grasp the ideas in either White's book or his own.

Critical success did not make writing any easier for Avi. Writing, especially writing well, remained a challenge, as Avi still suffered from dyslexia. He found that some of the mechanics of writing came more easily after he learned to use a computer spelling checker. In fact, when he realized that he could check his spelling electronically, he related that he felt teary-eyed with relief.[51]

The creative process did not become easier, however. After receiving the Newbery Honor for *The True Confessions of Charlotte Doyle*, Avi wrote

> I remain enthralled with the idea and act of writing, the capture of ideas, the design of plot, the finding and shaping of words, the struggle to discover the real truths that lurk within the hearts of imagined souls. How the persistent mix of pleasure and pain which comes from sitting in the semi-darkness that is my computer-lit study to make books which will attract readers. It's all that simple. It's all that complex. . . . I've begun a new book. Like every other time, I find myself hesitant, scared, worried. Oh, sure, I tell myself, I've been lucky before, but can I manage to write another readable book? I don't doubt that I share this fear with every other writer and artist.[52]

Children understood the character of Charlotte Doyle in many ways. One boy said, "Well, she's going to have trouble getting married." Another wrote to Avi, saying, "Charlotte lives in my heart! Forever!"[53]

Avi's novel Nothing But the Truth, *published in 1991, is subtitled "A Documentary Novel." The reader follows the plot through a series of memos, letters, speeches, journal entries, newspaper stories, and talk shows, as a simple incident, a student's decision to hum the national anthem instead of standing in "respectful silent attention," turns into a national scandal. Avi received his second Newbery Honor award for* Nothing But the Truth.

6

Awards and Experiments

NOTHING BUT THE TRUTH

AVI WROTE IN many different forms and genres during his years in Providence. A daring experiment with form, *Nothing But the Truth*, was published in 1991. The book tells the story of Phillip Malloy, a student at Harrison High School, who was suspended for a minor act of defiance—humming during a taped rendition of the "Star Spangled Banner," when he was supposed to stand in respectful silence. To tell the story, Avi created fictional diaries, memos, transcripts of telephone calls, radio shows, newspaper stories, interviews, and letters.

Avi called the form a "documentary novel," that is, one made up of documents that related to the events that occurred in Phillip's life. There is no narration. Descriptions are limited to what is quoted in the documents that form the novel. Different drafts of memos are used, as Phillip's suspension escalates into a full-blown media crisis with both Phillip and Mrs. Narwin, his teacher, at the epicenter. From one memo to the next, and from one newspaper article to the next, tiny inaccuracies are repeated and magnified out of proportion. Themes of patriotism, communication, exploitation, and the child's place in an adult world are all examined as the school's disciplinary action against Phillip's allegedly patriotic act comes to the attention of a school board candidate, and from him, to the media.

The novel began with two questions. The first question is asked of witnesses in court, "Do you swear to tell the truth, the whole truth, and nothing but the truth?" The second question is, "Does anyone say no?" About these questions, Avi wrote, "If someone said they would not tell the truth in court, we would believe them. Yet risking being found in contempt of court, everyone says 'yes' without thought, even without option. In short, we are all required to lie even as we swear to tell the truth. These two questions plunge readers immediately into the thematic depths of the novel: Truth is elusive; the truthteller, unreliable; and the system, corrupt."[54]

After the book was published, Avi learned that teachers, principals, and school administrators including district superintendents were passing the book around among themselves, claiming that the incident in the book had happened at their school. He wrote in the preface to the 2003 edition of the book,

When *Nothing But the Truth* was first published, I had trouble getting a reaction from the people it was written for: kids. Teachers were taking the book and passing it around among themselves, insisting that their principals, assistant principals, and superintendents read it. . . . It got so that when I spoke to groups of teachers about the book, I took to asking, "Has anyone NOT heard of such an incident happening in your schools?" No one ever raised a hand.[55]

In an interesting coincidence, a teacher at a school named Harrison High gave Avi a sheet of letterhead from her real-life school. The logo on the real letterhead was the same lamp of learning as the one that appeared on the fictional stationary in Avi's novel. More coincidences occurred. A school principal asked Avi if someone had given Avi the principal's own memos to use in the book. Avi's creation of such realistic details in his book started with his experiences during school visits. He was often taken to the teacher's lounge when he had time to wait between presentations in different classes. As he wrote,

It's here that teachers find time for a moment of relaxation, a flash of quiet, or an exchange with another teacher about what might be going on in the building that day.

And there I sit, listening to it all.

It's wonderful how much you can learn just by being quiet and listening. Sometimes you even learn the truth—or what seems to be the truth.[56]

Nothing But the Truth garnered Avi his second Newbery Honor award, plus a string of additional awards, including the *Boston Globe-Horn Book* Award, an Editors' Choice Award from the magazine *Booklist*, the New York State

Readers Award, an American Library Association Notable citation, and many others.

More experiments with form came after *Nothing But the Truth*. *"Who Was that Masked Man, Anyway?"* was told completely in dialogue. *Beyond the Western Sea, Books 1 & 2* were Victorian cliffhangers. *City of Light, City of Dark* had the subtitle *A Comic Book Novel*, and used a comic book format to tell a tale about the forces of good and evil battling above, below, and upon the island of Manhattan.[57]

Avi's artistic life brought him more awards and recognition; however, his personal life did not mirror his professional life. His father never acknowledged his successful writing career, even though Avi eventually published over fifty books and won many major awards. When Avi first learned that his disability had been diagnosed as a child, he asked his father why they had never told him about dyslexia. His father said, "It was your mother's decision." Avi felt this statement was a reflection of the roles his parents often assumed. His mother made most of the decisions concerning the children. Unfortunately, Avi's mother had died, and so he was unable to ask her about her decision. He felt that possibly it was a reflection of the times in which he grew

Did you know...

Avi's physical location has influenced the settings in his books. After he moved to Providence, Rhode Island, Avi wrote several books that were set in the past in Providence. After he moved to Colorado, Avi wrote several historical novels set in the past in Colorado and the West.

up or perhaps the result of an out-dated belief that having a disability was a private matter.

His own experience of parenting made him wonder about his parents' decision, in an unusual way. He was an active, involved parent. One of his sons, Kevin, shared his learning disability. Avi supported his son, met with Kevin's teachers, and did everything possible to encourage his son in school. Yet when Kevin grew up and was choosing a career, he did not consider becoming a writer. He said to Avi, "I can't. I have dyslexia." Avi, who had never had the label "dyslexia" applied to him as a child, grew up wanting to be a writer. It seemed ironic that his son felt the profession was closed to him.[58]

Avi's second marriage foundered. Realizing that they were not suited for each other, Avi and Coppélia separated and later divorced.

COLORADO

As part of his efforts to promote his books and increase his sales, Avi made many visits to schools and bookstores across the country. In 1996, he waited at the Denver Airport for a bookstore representative to pick him up. He was on a book tour, and an autographing was scheduled for the next day at a bookstore in Denver. Avi waited and waited. No one from the bookstore came to meet him.

Avi called the bookstore the next day and learned that his visit was completely unexpected. The bookstore had recently hired a new manager. The original manager who had arranged Avi's visit, and who was supposed to advertise the visit in the newspapers and in local schools, had not communicated with the new manager about Avi's visit. None of the publicity had gone out about the event. Only the new manager and her three children showed up for

Avi's book signing. The manager's name was Linda Wright. She and Avi talked for hours.

"It was love at first sight," said Avi.[59] He soon moved to Colorado.

Linda had worked in information technology, marketing, bookselling, and publishing. She and Avi planned to marry soon. In Colorado, marriages do not have to be performed by a minister or government official. Two people sign a marriage license and send it in to have their marriage registered. Avi and Linda went to a beautiful spot in the mountains, said their wedding vows, and signed the marriage license. Two weeks later, they got it back. They had signed it in the wrong place.

Interestingly, Linda's mother had suffered from the childhood disease that was widely feared during Avi's boyhood. Linda's mother had contracted polio. When she became pregnant with Linda, she had difficulty breathing, and she had to be placed in an iron lung. Linda was actually born in an iron lung, two months prematurely. At the time, many babies born so early did not survive, or had permanent, disabling injuries such as blindness. Linda not only survived, but grew up to become an active, creative person with an excellent career that ranged from high technology to bookselling to working with Avi on an exciting new concept that would bring stories to readers through their daily newspapers. The concept was called Breakfast Serials.

BREAKFAST SERIALS

Together, Avi and Linda began working on an idea to bring fiction to young readers in an unusual way. In the nineteenth century, fiction appeared in magazines and newspapers everywhere. Called serials, this kind of installment fiction brought fame to many novelists, including Charles Dickens,

George Elliot, and Thomas Hardy. Avi remembered reading serials in the *New York Herald Tribune* as a boy.[60]

In Avi's plan, a chapter of a story would appear once a week in the newspaper. He called his company "Breakfast Serials," making a pun on breakfast cereals. The pun, humorous in intent, underlined the importance of beginning the day with both healthy food and healthy reading. Waking up to a good breakfast, the most important meal, was joined to waking up to a good read, the most important brain activity of the day.

Avi's first book for the series was *Keep Your Eye on Amanda*, which appeared in the *Colorado Springs Gazette Tribune*. The story was inspired by a nighttime visit to Avi's house by a set of noisy raccoons. The first chapter ran on October 3, 1996, and the series continued for twenty-one weeks. The *Denver Post* asked to look at the story and accepted it for publication. One by one, other newspapers began to ask for serialized fiction. Some of the newspapers saw their circulation increase over sixty percent on days when the serials ran.[61]

Breakfast Serial's company goal was to motivate aliterates (people who can read, but lack the desire do so on a regular basis) to begin reading again. Avi and Linda saw aliteracy as a growing threat to education and, ultimately, to children's lifelong enjoyment of reading, to their ability to think creativity, and to continue to grow intellectually. As noted on the website for Breakfast Serials,

The Washington Post reports that our country is reading printed versions of books, magazines, and newspapers less and less. In 1991, more than half of all Americans read a half-hour or more every day. By 1999, that quantity had dropped significantly. *The Post* further adds that "aliteracy is

. . . like an invisible liquid, seeping through our culture, nigh impossible to pinpoint or defend against. It's the kid who spends hours and hours with video games instead of books. . . ." It's 50 percent of the general public—young and old.[62]

As Linda Wright wrote on the company's website, "We use the descriptor *books unbound* to refer to a traditional literary form—the serial novel—in a new way. Breakfast Serials extends that traditional form and function to create a twenty-first-century narrative experience. Our serials are great can't-put-it-down stories that readers anticipate with weekly pleasure—a desire for more to come. Hence, our literature is unbound, not just in form, but in the boundless way readers experience it."[63]

Avi and Linda signed up a virtual who's who of children's literature as their writers. From old friends like Betty Miles (author of *HEY! I'M READING!*, and the person to whom Avi had dedicated *Nothing But the Truth*) and Katherine Patterson (author of Newbery Award-winning books *Bridge to Terabithia* and *Jacob Have I Loved*) to newcomer Ji-li Jiang (whose first book, *Red Scarf Girl*, was published in 1997), Breakfast Serials was committed to publishing literature, written and illustrated by award-winning authors and artists, that children would look forward to reading.

Avi became chairman of the board of Breakfast Serials, while Linda served as president. The idea proved to be an overwhelming success, reaching ten million Americans. Avi cited three main reasons for the success of Breakfast Serials:

1. Although people in general are very busy, a small investment of time can be made, if future rewards are anticipated—an assumption of serial reading. One of the

anticipated rewards is learning what happens next in the forthcoming installment of the series.

2. Breakfast Serials provide print literature that is accessible and convenient because it's published in the local newspapers.

3. Breakfast Serials creates a dynamic reading experience that is social, something to talk about and enjoy with others. Serial reading and publishing are never separate from our everyday context of life. Unlike the private, contemplative read of a book, in which a reader invests long periods of time, serial reading forces us to leave a story and return to the complexities of life after one chapter. In the space *between* installments, readers talk about the characters, predict what's to come, and enrich the imagined story with our everyday experiences. When readers begin the next installment of the story, they bring all this richness to the continuing story.[64]

About Breakfast Serials, a critic wrote, "For me, the most exciting thing about the entire project is that serialization—with its built-in cliff-hanger endings—has got kids talking about books, speculating about what will happen next, and waiting anxiously to read the next installment. And research consistently shows that one way to excite the interest of reluctant readers in books is to start them talking about the reading they're doing."[65]

Discussing Breakfast Serials became a shared, multi-generational experience that both adults and children enjoyed. In an age of video games, movies, hundreds of channels on television, computers, and the Internet, the simple act of reading a story with parents, grandparents, or friends proved to be both enjoyable and intellectually stimulating.

In his book The Mayor of Central Park, *Avi writes about baseball, one of his childhood passions. The story's hero, Oscar Westerwit, is a squirrel and manager of the Central Park Green Sox baseball team, who must defend his territory from a pack of bad rats. The pack is headed by Big Daddy Duds, who wants to take over Oscar's territory.*

Newbery Award and New Challenges

SEPTEMBER 11, 2001

DURING THE PERIOD that Avi spent working on Breakfast Serials, the September 11, 2001, terrorist attacks occurred. Avi reported that he felt unbearably sad after the attacks. He was comforted when he heard a program on National Public Radio about people's feelings during the weeks following September 11. He realized that his feelings of sadness mirrored the country's national state of depression as described on the radio program. He tried to work on a serious book about the tragedy, but found that the work was so forced that he went back to a more lighthearted work in progress, a humorous book called *The Mayor of Central Park.*

Avi's work with children proved to be a further aid in recovering from the effects of September 11. A seventh-grade English teacher wrote and told him that her students were reading much more than they had in the past. She felt that reading books like Avi's, about serious topics, where the children made up their own minds about the ambiguities that Avi had left in his works, comforted them after the terrorist attacks. Children gained strength, solace, and comfort from his works, and Avi in turn felt a sense of relief in knowing that his books were helping children in such vital areas.

CRISPIN

Always one to work on many projects at once, Avi continued to write prolifically, publishing a book, or sometimes two, every year. He had been interested in medieval history for many years. He was fascinated by the way the modern era of liberty and the belief in individual achievement based on personal abilities arose out of a time when birth determined social status. He learned that even in the Middle Ages, a serf who ran away from his master and lived in a free town for a year and a day became free. He immersed himself in medieval culture and began working on a story about a young boy named Crispin who was forced to leave his small village. After reading his first draft, his editor, Donna Bray, wrote,

> I was transported immediately to the narrator's small English village. I felt the damp rains, smelled the rotting wood and leaves thick on the forest floor, and most of all experienced the monotonous, backbreaking, hopeless lives of the villagers,

who worked from dawn to dusk day after day, for no personal gain. Crispin's change of fortune was dramatic, his triumph immensely satisfying. And the main characters were vivid and memorable. Once again, Avi had managed to inhabit a completely foreign time and place, and make it at once authentic and accessible.[66]

Although Bray loved the manuscript, there was still work to be done. The book needed revisions, and there were many details, even the title, still to be thought about or changed. The beginning was rewritten so many times that Bray confessed, "Did I dare ask him to revisit it *yet again?* But he was never in the least unwilling, and in fact seemed energized to start over and get it right. For Avi, the process of rewriting seemed to be more than just fixing what was written—it was discovery. It is this sense of curiosity and discovery, of the writing being as much of an adventure as the story, that comes through in his books and makes them immediate and engaging."[67]

Crispin's development as a character, and the drastic changes he goes through during his transformation from a downtrodden peasant to a boy who believed in his own potential, reflect Avi's belief that fictional characters must act within the context of their own characters. Avi wrote,

Did you know...

Avi's original goal was to publish at least six books in his lifetime. *Crispin: The Cross of Lead* was Avi's fiftieth book, and it was not his last book. He published more than nine times as many books as he originally hoped to.

"For fictional characters to be believable, they must behave and speak in realistic ways. They also have to be consistent: Throughout the story, they must act in ways that fit the personality the author has established for them. Even if they undergo big changes, they have to change in believable ways."[68]

In 2002, the book Avi had been writing with Bray as his editor was published. The title they finally chose was *Crispin: Cross of Lead*. Avi expressed early fears about the book to Bray, cautioning her not to get her hopes up about it. Bray wrote,

> When I said something about being anxious to finally get the book out into the world and see the reviews, he gently warned me against getting my hopes up. His books always receive mixed reviews, he told me. People who love his animal stories may not love his historical fiction, and those who admire his historical fiction don't cotton to his humorous or more experimental work.
>
> I was a bit surprised. Was an author comforting *me* about reviews—*in advance?*.... [Avi] did once share with me an anecdote about Sir Laurence Olivier's response to Charlton Heston regarding a play they had done together. Heston said, "Well, I guess you've just got to forget the bad reviews." To which Olivier is reported to have replied, "No, you've got to forget the good ones."[69]

Avi was to have the best of good reviews to use in order to try out Olivier's advice. On January 27, 2003, he was working at his computer before daybreak. The phone rang with a call from the American Library Association. *Crispin* had won the highest award for a children's book, the Newbery Medal.

In his acceptance speech, Avi wrote,

. . . it appears I must answer the question that I quickly discovered is part of the established ritual attached to this prize: how did it feel to win?

I was in Philadelphia for most of ALA Midwinter, introducing another book. I was sick with some kind of flu and dared not eat for three days. It was bitterly cold, too, so I spent as much time as I could in my hotel room with a blanket around my shoulders working on a laptop on one project or another. The image of the lonely, sick writer in his garret almost fits.

When I was obliged to take part in proceedings and chanced upon Newbery committee members, they turned away in haste, eyes averted—as if I were some pariah. How humiliating! How depressing! I was so eager to get home I arrived at the airport two hours early. Why stay for Monday's announcements and become even more depressed? Had I not recently worried that *Crispin* had not done as well as I thought it might? Had not my wife said to me as I left for Philadelphia, "If you think you might win an award, stay another day." And had I not answered, "Honey, if I were really smart I'd stay home and write something good."

Where was I when the call came? I was sitting where every self-respecting writer who is also a parent should be at five-thirty in the morning: working at my desk, editing my college-age daughter's application for a summer job.

In truth, when I got the news I was surprised, elated, humbled, and deeply moved. Once I accepted the news—it took a bit to believe—what did I do? I burst into tears. It required some time for me to sort out the meaning of those tears. Were they tears of grief? No. Tears of joy? Not really.

I have thought hard: The only vaguely comparable moment of ecstasy in my writing career occurred when I had hooked up my first computer and discovered how to use a spell checker.

Indeed, those were tears of relief. My world was telling me an extraordinary simple but powerful thing: I had been recognized as a good writer.

Why relief? Because, friends, writing is hard. And writing very well is very hard. Never believe any writer who suggests otherwise. Scratch the surface of any successful author. Just below—in fetal position, sucking a thumb—is an insecure writer. For all of us writing well is always a struggle.[70]

ADVICE FOR WRITERS

Struggle though it has been, writing well has always been Avi's goal. For young writers, he offers five secrets that he has found lead to good writing:

One: Write! It's not writing until it's on the paper. Story telling is a great art, but it is not story writing.

Two: Rewrite! No one ever writes anything well the first time. The first draft can not be the last draft. (I rewrite my work fifty to sixty times, or more.) Here's a tip: read your first draft, and if you think it's good, you are in trouble. But if you read it and you see it's not that good, you are in great shape— to get going. The more you rewrite the better your writing will be.

Three: Write for a reader. Maybe you understand what you have written, but the writer's job is to have the reader understand it. Keep in mind: writers don't write writing, they write reading.

Four: Listen. Read your work out loud (pencil in hand) and it will let you hear your own writing. It will almost improve itself.

Five: Read, read, read. Reading is the key to good writing. The more you read, the better the writer you can be. You can NEVER read too much.[71]

Reading has often been part of the advice that professional writers give to novices. For Avi, reading was the first of his list of secrets, but not because reading was easy. "I believe deeply that the hardest part of writing is reading. One simply cannot be a writer unless he learns to read well. One writes and is called a writer, but one has to be able to read what's been written *as* a reader. It is the response as reader that enables the writer to make the necessary adjustments and changes to the story. For me, it's a totally intuitive process."[72]

For Avi, writing for children requires additional thought and attention. He wrote,

I believe that we who write for children have a number of obligations. The first is to write as well as we can. The second is to be honest. The third is that we hold out a vision of achievement. It does not matter if the vision is happy or tragic, witty or somber. What matters is that we proclaim that life is worth living, that the struggle we undertake together must be one that fulfills the promise of our selves. I try to write from the heart. A good children's book is a book of promises, and promises are meant to be kept.[73]

In describing the process of writing, and explaining his second secret of good writing, Avi has said,

I joke to myself that I write very slowly quickly. That describes this endless revision. Partly, it has to do with dyslexia. . . . I work on the computer and then will go over the computer copy many, many times. Then I'll print it out and go over the hard copy. Then I insert the changes from the printed text back into the computer and start all over again.

Some of the things I do: I take notes. I will write and describe the character in the text and then separate these out, put them on a separate sheet of paper and develop character sketches. I don't do them as a prefatory step to writing. Then I keep these by my side while I write about that character. Occasionally I will glance at the character sketch as a way of reminding myself.[74]

NEW CHALLENGES

Avi and his friend Rachel Veil invented a new way to work when they started the novel *Never Mind!* as a collaboration. The book was a story of twins, with Avi writing the chapters from the boy twin's point of view, and Rachel writing the chapters from the girl twin's point of view. The work began when they talked about a book that Avi thought about writing with his twin sister Emily. Rachel wrote,

I was moaning and complaining about the book I was trying not to write at the time. You said it sounded like a book you had wanted to write with your sister. I got you talking about it hoping it would jolt me out of my [writers'] block. . . . It was always my fantasy, while in the mucky middle of writing a book, that some bookmaker's elves would come and just write the next chapter. Not do all the work, but jolt me to a new place, surprise me. I'd get this book [*Never Mind!*] back from Avi, and read from page one. Stuff had been changed, improved, and then there was a new chapter at the end which was often a cliffhanger: "So I picked up the phone and could not believe whose voice I heard." [I wondered] Whose voice? So I'd call Avi [and ask him]: "Whose voice?" He'd say, "I don't know. Up to you." So I'd be like, "Oh yeah?" And [I would] try to leave him in the same lurch.[75]

Published in 2004, *Never Mind!* received critical appraisals that called it hysterically funny and over-the-top, yet completely realistic.[76]

The year 2005 was the fiftieth anniversary of high school graduation for Avi. The boy who almost flunked out, the boy who was told he could not, in his wildest dreams, ever achieve his goal to become a writer, had the opportunity to look back over his career. Not only had he become a writer, despite the challenges of dyslexia, he had become a prolific and highly-regarded award-winning writer in the field of children's literature. And there were more books, more ideas, and more challenges yet to come.

1   Winarski, Diana. "Avi on Fiction," *Teaching K–8*, September 1997, p. 62.

2   Interview with Avi, May 27, 2004.

3   Quoted in Markham, Lois, *Avi*. Santa Barbara, CA: The Learning Works, 1996, p. 6.

4   Broderick, Kathleen. "Talking With Avi," *Book Links*, March 1997, p. 58.

5   Benson, Sonia. "Avi," *Something about the Author,* Volume 71, Gale, 1992, p. 9.

6   Markham, Lois. *Avi*, p. 42

7   Interview with Avi, May 27, 2004.

8   Interview with Avi, May 27, 2004.

9   Interview with Avi, May 27, 2004.

10 Benson, Sonia. "Avi," p. 9.

11 Interview with Avi, May 27, 2004.

12 Quoted in Harvey, Mary, "Advice from Avi," *Scholastic Scope*, Volume 51, Issue 11, January 24, 2003.

13 *http://www.lrei.org/whoweare/ history_philosophy.html*.

14 Markham, Lois. *Avi*, p. 48.

15 Avi. "All that Glitters," *Horn Book Magazine*, September/October 1987, p. 570.

16 Benson, Sonia. "Avi," pp. 9–10.

17 Markham, Lois. *Avi*, p. 51.

18 Background and information about the Civil Rights Act of 1964 may be found here: *www.congresslink.org/civil/ essay.html*. CongressLink provides information about the U.S. Congress—how it works, its members and leaders, and the public policies it produces. The site also hosts lesson plans and reference and historical materials related to congressional topics.

19 Bloom, Susan P., and Cathryn M. Mercier. *Presenting Avi*. New York, NY: Twayne Publishers, 1997, p. 152.

20 Marinak, B.A. "Author Profile Avi," *Book Report*, Mar/April 92 (Volume 10, number 5).

21 Interview with Avi, May 27, 2004.

22 Benson, Sonia. "Avi," p. 10.

23 Ibid.

24 Bloom, Susan P., and Cathryn M. Mercier. *Presenting Avi*, p. 6.

25 Markham, Lois. *Avi*, p. 61.

26 Bloom, Susan P., and Cathryn M. Mercier. *Presenting Avi*, p. xiv.

27 Ibid., p. 35.

28 Avi, "All that Glitters," p. 571.

29 Benson, Sonia. "Avi," p. 10.

30 Benson, Sonia. "Avi," p. 10.

31 Fischer, quoted in Bloom and Mercier, *Presenting Avi*, p. 8.

32 Broderick, Kathleen. "Talking With Avi," p. 59.

33 Benson, Sonia. "Avi," p. 10.

34 Avi and Betty Miles. "School Visits: The Author's Viewpoint," *School Library Journal,* January, 1987, p. 21.

35 Ibid., p. 22.

36 Bloom, Susan P., and Cathryn M. Mercier. *Presenting Avi*, p. xii.

37 Avi. "All that Glitters," *The Horn Book*, September/October 1987, pp. 575–76.

38 Avi. "On Historical Fiction," Children's Book Council, Author/Illustrator Archives, *www.cbcbooks.org*.

39 Avi. "Curriculum Administrator Talks with Avi," *Curriculum Administrator*, Vol. 31, Issue 3, October, 1996.

40 Cooper, Ilene. "Avi," *Booklist*, May 2002, p. 1609.

41 Ibid.

42 Interview with Avi, May 27, 2004.

43 Benson, Sonia. "Avi," p. 9.

44 Bloom, Susan P., and Cathryn M. Mercier. *Presenting Avi*, p. 150.

45 Ibid., p. 63.

46 Ibid., p. 63.

47 Ibid., p. 64.

48 Halls, Kelly Milner. "The Magic of Avi," *Smart Writers*, May 2004, *www.smartwriters.com/index.2ts?page=writersonwriting&sub=item&wrtid=56*.

49 Bloom, Susan P., and Cathryn M. Mercier. *Presenting Avi*, p. 110.

50 Avi. "Boston Globe-Horn Book Award Acceptance Speech," *Horn Book*, January–February, 1992, p. 24.

51 Avi. Newbery Acceptance Speech, June 22, 2003, *www.avi-writer.com*.

52 Avi. "Boston Globe-Horn Book Award Acceptance Speech," p. 25.

53 Ibid.

54 Bloom, Susan P., and Cathryn M. Mercier. *Presenting Avi*, p. 81.

55 Avi, *Nothing But the Truth*. New York: Orchard Books, 2003, Preface.

56 Ibid.

57 Bloom, Susan P., and Cathryn M. Mercier. *Presenting Avi*, p. 70.

58 Interview with Avi, May 27, 2004.

59 Interview with Avi, May 27, 2004.

60 Cart, Michael. "Breakfast Serials," *Booklist*, Vol. 95, Issue 9–10, Jan. 1, 1999.

61 Ibid.

62 *www.breakfastserials.com/commentsAliteracy.asp*.

63 Ibid.

64 Ibid.

65 Cart, Michael. "Breakfast Serials."

66 Bray, Donna. "Avi," *Horn Book*, July/August 2003, p. 417.

67 Ibid., p. 415.

68 Eftehkar, Judy. "The Transformation of Charlotte Doyle," *Writing*, Vol. 25, Issue 5, Feb/Mar 2003.

69 Ibid., p. 418.

70 The full text of Avi's acceptance speech for the Newbery Medal is on his website, *www.avi-writer.com*.

71 *www.avi-writer.com/5_secrets_writing.html*.

72 Bloom, Susan P., and Cathryn M. Mercier. *Presenting Avi*, p. 152.

73 Halls, Kelly Milner. "The Magic of Avi."

74 Bloom, Susan P., and Cathryn M. Mercier. *Presenting Avi*, p. 152.

75 Avi and Rachel Veil. "Never Mind!" HarperCollins Interview, *http://www.harpercollins.com/catalog/book_interview_xml.asp?isbn=0060543159*.

76 Mitnick, Eva. "Never Mind!" *School Library Journal*, May 2004. *http://reviews.schoollibraryjournal.com/bd.aspx?isbn=0060543140&pub=sl*.

1937 Avi Wortis born on December 23 in Manhattan, New York.

1938 Wortis family moves to Brooklyn, New York.

1942 Avi begins elementary school.

1951 Avi transfers from Stuyvesant High School to Elizabeth Irwin High School.

1954 Avi receives tutoring from Ella Ratner.

1955 Avi decides to become a writer. He graduates from high school and goes to Antioch College in Ohio.

1957 Avi transfers to the University of Wisconsin.

1959 Avi graduates with a double major in history and playwriting. He remains at the University of Wisconsin to study playwriting.

1960 Avi wins the University of Wisconsin playwriting award. He moves to San Francisco to become the playwright-in-residence at the World Theater.

1961 Avi returns to New York.

1962 Avi begins working at the New York Public Library.

1963 Avi marries Joan Gainer.

1964 Avi receives his master's degree in library science from Columbia University.

1966 Avi's son Shaun is born.

1968 Avi and his family spend nine months in England. Avi's son Kevin is born.

1970 Avi and his family return to New York. Avi accepts a position as librarian at Trenton State College in Trenton, NJ. Avi's first book, *Things That Sometimes Happen: Thirty Very Short Stories for the Very Young*, is published.

1972 *Snail Tale* is published.

1975 Avi's first novel, *No More Magic*, is published.

1976 Avi and his family move to New Hope, PA.

1982 Avi and Joan are divorced.

1983 Avi marries Coppélia Kahn. They move to Providence, RI. Avi writes full-time.

1991 *The True Confessions of Charlotte Doyle* receives the Newbery Award.

1992 *Nothing But the Truth* receives the Newbery Award.

1995 Avi separates and then divorces Coppélia and moves to Colorado.

1996 Avi and Linda Wright cofound Breakfast Serials, a company that arranges to have fiction for children published in serial format in daily newspapers around the country.

1998 Avi marries Linda.

2003 *Crispin: The Cross of Lead* wins the Newbery Award.

RAGWEED, POPPY AND RYE, ERETH'S BIRTHDAY, POPPY'S RETURN (2005)

These four books are set in Dimwood Forest. They concern the adventures of deer mice Ragweed, Poppy, and Rye, with their friend Ereth, a porcupine. The mice and porcupine face a number of woodland enemies, and experience both loss and love as they encounter beavers, cats, and a great horned owl, among others.

BRIGHT SHADOW

A servant girl named Morwenna receives all the wishes that are left in the kingdom from a dying magician. She must make life or death decisions about how to use the wishes and she knows her life will end when she uses the last one. Since there are only five wishes left to begin with, her choices are difficult and heart-rending.

CRISPIN: THE CROSS OF LEAD

A boy named Crispin must leave his home village after he is accused of murder. He meets a traveling performer named Bear, who befriends him. Bear teaches Crispin how to make a living as a performer and how to believe in himself. Crispin learns who his father was and that his station in life is based on his own worth, not on his birth.

THE FIGHTING GROUND

A boy named Jonathan joins the civilian militia to take back the town of Trenton during the Revolutionary War. He is captured, but is befriended by his captors. He learns that war is not glorious.

NOTHING BUT THE TRUTH

Phillip Malloy, a high school student, hums during the "Star Spangled Banner," when he is supposed to stand in respectful silence. His teacher sends him to the office, where the vice-principal suspends him. He becomes a symbol for patriotism when his story is taken up by a school board candidate, who broadcasts it to the media in the hope of bolstering his campaign. Phillip, misunderstood and unhappy, transfers to another school, where he is asked to sing the national anthem to show his patriotism. The ending is ironic and underscores how difficult it is to tell the truth, the whole truth, and nothing but the truth.

TRUE CONFESSIONS OF CHARLOTTE DOYLE

Charlotte Doyle embarks for America to join her family in 1832. She witnesses the cruelty of the ship's captain and sides with the crew in a mutiny. She learns important truths about herself and about the value of each person regardless of their social position.

"WHO WAS THAT MASKED MAN, ANYWAY?"

Frankie is a boy who lives in New York during World War II. He lives his life through radio shows and uses phrases from them constantly. Frankie gets into trouble at school and at home, but finds a clever way out of his difficulties using what he learned from the Lone Ranger's radio show.

BOOKS

1970 *Things That Sometimes Happen*

1972 *Snail Tale*

1975 *No More Magic*

1977 *Captain Grey*

1978 *Emily Upham's Revenge*

1979 *Night Journeys*

1980 *History of Helpless Harry*

1980 *Man From the Sky*

1981 *Encounter at Easton, Who Stole the Wizard of Oz?*, and *A Place Called Ugly*

1982 *Sometimes I Think I Hear My Name*

1983 *Shadrach's Crossing*

1984 *The Fighting Ground*

1984 *S.O.R. Losers* and *Devil's Race*

1985 *Bright Shadow*

1986 *Wolf Rider*

1987 *Romeo and Juliet—Together (and Alive!)At Last*

1988 *Something Upstairs*

1989 *The Man Who Was Poe*

1990 *The True Confessions of Charlotte Doyle*

1991 *Nothing But The Truth* and *Windcatcher*

1992 *"Who Was That Masked Man, Anyway?"* and *Blue Heron*

1993 *City of Light, City of Dark*

1993 *Punch With Judy*

1994 *The Barn* and *The Bird, The Frog and the Light*

1995 *Poppy* and *Tom, Babette & Simon*

1996 *Keep Your Eye on Amanda, Beyond the Western Sea. Book One: The Escape from Home, Beyond the Western Sea. Book Two: Lord Kirkle's Money, When I Was Your Age*, and *"What Ruby Saw"*

1997   *Finding Providence, What Do Fish Have To Do With Anything?, Amanda Joins the Circus!,* and *From One Experience To Another*

1998   *Perloo the Bold* and *Poppy & Rye*

1999   *Midnight Magic, Ragweed, Abigail Takes the Wheel,* and *Second Sight*

2000   *The Secret School, The Christmas Rat,* and *Ereth's Birthday*

2001   *The Good Dog, The Secret School, "Don't You Know There's A War On?", Prairie School* and *The Color of Absence*

2002   *Things That Sometimes Happen* (Revised) and *Crispin: The Cross of Lead*

2003   *The Mayor Of Central Park, Silent Movie,* and *911: The Book of Help*

2004   *The End of the Beginning, Never Mind!* (Written with Rachel Vail), and *Tripping Over the Lunch Lady*

2005   *The Book with No Words* and *Poppy's Return*

ARTICLES

Regular reviewer for the *Library Journal, School Library Journal,* 1965–1973.

"Children's Literature: The American Revolution," in *Top of the News,* Winter 1977.

"When Authors Visit Schools: A Symposium," in *Children's Literature in Education,* Autumn 1980.

"Some thoughts of the YA World," in *VOYA,* October 1982.

"Writing Books for Children," in *The Writer,* March 1982.

"Reviewing the Reviewers," in *School Library Journal,* March 1986.

"School Visits: The Author's Viewpoint" (written with Betty Miles), in *School Library Journal,* January 1987.

"All That Glitters," in *Horn Book,* September 1987.

"Robert Lawson," in Jane M. Bingham (ed), *Writers for Children,* New York: Scribner's, 1987.

Acceptance Speech for the *Boston Globe-Horn Book* Award (for *The True Confessions of Charlotte Doyle*), in *Horn Book,* January 1992.

"The Child in Children's Literature," in *Horn Book*, February 1993.

"Young People, Books and the Right to Read," in *Journal of Youth Services in Libraries*, Spring 1993.

"Seeing Through the I," in *ALAN Review*, Spring 1993.

"I Can Read, I Can Read!" in *Horn Book*, March/April 1994.

Acceptance Speech for the Boston Globe-Horn Book Award (for *Poppy*), in *Horn Book*, January 1997.

"Writing Backward but Looking Forward," in *Signal*, Summer 1999.

Acceptance Speech for the 2003 Newbery Award, in *Horn Book*, July–August 2003.

"A Sense of Story," in *Voices from The Middle*, September 2003.

POPPY

In the Tales of Dimwood Forest (*Ragweed, Poppy and Rye, Ereth's Birthday,* and *Poppy's Return*), Poppy the deer mouse demonstrates that her courage belies her small size.

ERETH

In the Tales of Dimwood Forest (*Ragweed, Poppy and Rye, Ereth's Birthday,* and *Poppy's Return*), Ereth the porcupine shows that his grouchiness conceals a nurturing heart.

BEAR

In *Crispin: Cross of Lead*, Bear teaches Crispin how to survive and value himself.

CHARLOTTE DOYLE

In the *True Confessions of Charlotte Doyle*, Charlotte joins a mutiny aboard the *Seahawk*.

CRISPIN

In *Crispin: Cross of Lead*, Crispin learns about his own value after he is accused of murder and is forced to run away from home.

FRANKIE

In *"Who Was That Masked Man, Anyway?"* Frankie solves a mystery using what he learned from *The Lone Ranger* radio show.

MORWENNA

In *Bright Shadow*, Morwenna receives the remaining five wishes of the kingdom from a dying wizard.

PHILLIP MALLOY

In *Nothing But the Truth*, Phillip is suspended from school for humming during the "Star Spangled Banner."

THE BARN: American Library Association Notable, 1995; International Reading Association Teacher's Choice, 1995; Bank Street Children's Books of the year, "Outstanding," 1994; Starred Review, *Booklist*, 1994 (*Focus Review*); American Bookseller, Pick of the Lists, 1994; New York Public Library, Best Books of the Year, 1994; *Booklist*, Best Books of the year, 1994; Editor's Choice, *Booklist*, 1994; Canadian Children's Book Council Choice, 1994; Voice Of Youth Advocates, Outstanding Book, 1994; ABC Children's Booksellers' Choice, 1995.

BEYOND THE WESTERN SEA: Best books for Young Adults, American Library Association, 1997; Notable, National Council of Social Studies/Children's Book Council, 1997; Starred Review, *Booklist*, 1996; Best Books of the Year, *Book Links*, 1996; Best Books of the Year, *Booklist*, 1996; New York Public Library, Best Books of the Year, 1996; Blue Ribbon, *The Bulletin of the Center for Children's Books*, 1997; Children's choice nominee, Vermont.

THE BIRD, THE FROG AND THE LIGHT: An American Booksellers Pick of the Lists, 1994; Bank Street Children's Books of the year, 1994

BLUE HERON: American Library Association Best Books for Young Adults, 1993; Starred Review, *Booklist*, 1992 (*Focus Review*); Pointed Review, *Kirkus Reviews*, 1992; New York Public Library, *Books for the Teen Age*, 1993.

CITY OF LIGHT, CITY OF DARK: Starred Review, *Publishers Weekly*, 1993; One of the Best Children's Books of the Year, *Publishers Weekly*, 1993; New York Public Library, *Books for the Teen Age*, 1994.

CRISPIN: THE CROSS OF LEAD: Newbery Medal, 2003; American Library Association Notable, 2003; Starred Review: *School Library Journal*; Starred Review, *Publishers Weekly*; Book Sense Top Ten; Best Children's Books of the year, 2003 list, Bank Street College of Education; Children's Choice nominee, Kansas; Children's Choice nominee, Vermont; Children's Choice nominee, Texas; Colorado Book award.

THE CHRISTMAS RAT: Starred Review, *School Library Journal*.

"DON'T YOU KNOW THERE'S A WAR ON?": Children's Choice nominee, Oklahoma; Children's Choice nominee, Missouri; Children's Choice nominee, Virginia.

EMILY UPHAM'S REVENGE: Special Award, Mystery Writers of America, 1979; Starred Review, *School Library Journal*, 1978; Book of the Month, PCRRT, 1978.

ENCOUNTER AT EASTON: Christopher Award, 1980; Starred Review, *School Library Journal*, 1980.

THE FIGHTING GROUND: O'Dell Award, Best Historical Fiction, 1984; American Library Association Notable, 1984; American Library Association Best Books for Young Adults, 1984; Bologna, International Book Fair, White Raven, 1984; Notable Children's Trade Books in Social Studies, 1984; Jefferson Cup Award Honor Book (Virginia Library Association), 1985; Book of the Month, PCRRT, 1984; Devil's Race; American Library Association Best Books Hi-Lo, 1984.

FINDING PROVIDENCE: Pick of the Lists, International Reading Association, 1997.

THE GOOD DOG: Rocky Mountain News, one of best books of the year, 2001; Children's Choice nominee, Pennsylvania.

HISTORY OF HELPLESS HARRY: Starred Review, *School Library Journal*, 1980; Starred Review, *Booklist*, 1980; Book of the Month, PCRRT, 1980.

MAN FROM THE SKY: International Reading Association Children's Choice, 1980; Starred Review, *Booklist*, 1980.

THE MAN WHO WAS POE: One Of the Best Books of Year, Library of Congress, 1990; Nominated, Best Juvenile Mystery of the Year, Mystery Writers of America, 1990; Notable Children's Book, National Council of Teachers of English, 1990; One of the Best Books of the Year, New York Public Library, 1989; Starred Review, *Booklist*, 1990 (*Focus Review*).

THE MAYOR OF CENTRAL PARK: Starred Review, *Publishers Weekly*, 2003.

MIDNIGHT MAGIC: Children's Choice award, Utah, 2002; Starred Review, *Publishers Weekly*, 2002; Young Adult Library Services Association Quick Pick, 2000; International Reading Association Children's Choice 2000; International Reading Association Teacher's Choice 2000; Children's Choice nominee, North Carolina; Children's Choice nominee, New Mexico; Children's Choice nominee, Florida.

NEVER MIND!: Starred Review, *Booklist*, 2004.

NIGHT JOURNEYS: School Library Journal Best Books Of The Year List, 1980; Starred Review, *School Library Journal*, 1979.

NO MORE MAGIC: Special Award, Mystery Writers of America, 1975.

NOTHING BUT THE TRUTH: Garden State Teen Award, 1995; Young Adult Library Services Association One of the Best Young Adults's from the Last 25 Years, 1994; Arizona Young Readers Award, 1994; New York State Readers Award, 1994; Newbery Honor Book, 1992; *Horn Book-Boston Globe* Award Honor Book, 1992; ALA Notable, 1992; Best Books for Young Adults 1992, Young Adult Services Division; Editors' Choice 1991, *Booklist*; One of the Best Books of 1991, *Hornbook*; One of the Best Books of 1991, *School Library Journal*; Best Books of 1991, *Publishers Weekly*; American Booksellers Children's Choice List, 1992; Best Books for Teens 1992, New York Public Library; National Council of Teachers of English Notable, Children's Trade Book in the Language Arts, 1992; Notable, National Council of Social Studies/Children's Book Council, 1991; Bulletin of the Center for Children's Books/Blue Ribbon Book; One of the Best Books of the Year, Banks St. Teachers College, 1992; Library Of Congress: Best Books for Children, 1992; Starred Review, *Booklist*, 1991; Starred Review, *Hornbook*, 1992; Starred Review, *School Library Journal*, 1991; Starred Review, *Bulletin for the Center of Children's Books*, 1991; Pointed Review, *Kirkus Reviews*, 1991; *Horn Book*, Fanfare Award, 1992.

PERLOO THE BOLD: Starred Review, *Publishers Weekly*; One of Top 10 Fantasy Novels for Youth, 1998-1999, Booklist; Children's Choice nominee, Oklahoma; Children's Choice nominee, New Mexico; Children's Choice nominee, Texas; Children's Choice nominee, Florida; Children's Choice nominee, Connecticut.

A PLACE CALLED UGLY: Starred Review, *School Library Journal*, 1981.

PRAIRIE SCHOOL: Oppenheim Toy Portfolio Gold Award, 2004.

ROMEO AND JULIET, TOGETHER (AND ALIVE!) AT LAST: American Library Association/Young Adult Services Division Recommended Book for Reluctant Readers, 1988; International Reading Association Children's Choice, 1988; Bank Street College Children's Book Committee, One of the Best Books of the Year, 1988; Wisconsin Children's Book Center, One of the Best Books of the Year, 1988; Starred Review, *Booklist*, 1987; A Child Study Association Book of the Year.

S.O.R. LOSERS: Parents' Choice, Remarkable, 1984; New York Public Library, Best Books, 1984; Book of the Month, PCRRT, 1984; Young Adult Services Division Recommended Book for the Reluctant Reader.

SECRET SCHOOL: International Reading Association-CBC Children's Choice Award 2002; Children's Literature Choice, 2002; *Smithsonian Magazine*, A Notable Book Of the year, 2001; Parent's Guide Media Awards, 2001; Children's Choice nominee, Kansas; Children's Choice nominee, South Carolina; Children's Choice nominee, California.

SHADRACH'S CROSSING: Special Award, Mystery Writers of America, 1983.

SILENT MOVIE: American Library Association Notable, 2004; Starred Review, *Booklist*, 2004.

SNAIL TALE: One of the Best Books of the Year, British Book Council, 1973.

SOMETHING UPSTAIRS: Young Adult Library Services Association Popular Paperbacks for Young Adults, 1999; Rhode Island Award, 1991; Florida Sunshine Award, 1992; California Young Readers Award, 1993; American Library Association Notable Recording, 1992 (Recorded Books, Inc.); One of the Best Books of Year, Library of Congress, 1989; Nominated, Best Juvenile Mystery of the Year, Mystery Writers of America, 1989.

TALES FROM DIMWOOD FOREST: 1. RAGWEED: Starred Review, *Publishers Weekly*; One of the Top Ten Fantasy Books of 1999, *Booklist*; Children's Choice nominee, North Carolina.

TALES FROM DIMWOOD FOREST: 2. POPPY: New Mexico's Children Choice Award, 1999; National Christian School Association, Crown Classic, 1998; Maryland's Children's Choice Award, 1998; *Horn Book-Boston Globe* Best Fiction Award, 1996; American Library Association Notable, 1996; Starred Review, *Publishers Weekly*, 1995; Starred Review, *Booklist*, 1995; *Booklist*, Best Books of the Year, 1995; One of the Best Books of 1995, School Library Journal; New York Public Library, Best Books of the Year, 1995; Book Links Salutes a Few Good Books, 1995; Nominated for twenty five state children's choice awards.

TALES FROM DIMWOOD FOREST: 3. POPPY AND RYE: Children's choice nominee, Vermont; Children's choice nominee, Illinois; Children's choice nominee, Pennsylvania; Children's choice nominee, New Mexico; Children's choice nominee, Iowa.

TALES FROM DIMWOOD FOREST: 4. ERETH'S BIRTHDAY: *Parent's Guide*, Outstanding Achievement, 2000; Children's Choice nominee, Texas; Children's Choice nominee, Nebraska; Children's Choice nominee, Georgia; Children's Choice nominee, Vermont; Children's Choice nominee, Missouri; Children's Choice nominee, Tennessee; Children's Choice nominee, Louisiana.

THINGS THAT SOMETIMES HAPPEN: Family Fun—Best Books of the Year, 2002.

TOM, BABETTE & SIMON: Starred Review, *Publishers Weekly*, 1955.

THE TRUE CONFESSIONS OF CHARLOTTE DOYLE: Association of Library Service —100 Books Kids Should Read, 2000; One Of The 100 Most Significant Children's' Books of the 20th Century, *School Library Journal*, 2000; Massachusetts Children's Choice Award, 1996; Florida Young Reader's Award, 1994; Utah, Young Adults Award, 1994; Newbery Honor Book, 1991; *Horn Book-Boston Globe* Award, 1991; American Library Association Notable, 1991; American Library Association Notable Recording (Recorded Books, Inc.), 1992; Best Books for Young Adults 1991, Young Adult Services Division; Editors' Choice 1990, *Booklist*; *Fanfare* 1991, *Horn Book*; One of the Best Books of 1990, *School Library Journal*; Best Books for Teens 1990, New York Public Library; National Council of Teachers of English Notable 1991 Children's Trade Book in the Language Arts; Lopez Memorial Foundation Award, 1990; One of the Best Books of 1990, Child Study Association; International Reading Association Children's Choice, 1990; Library Of Congress: 100 Books for Children, 1991; *English Journal*'s Honor List, 1991; Starred Review, *Booklist*, 1990; Starred Review, *Horn Book*, 1991; Starred Review, *School Library Journal*, 1990; Pointed Review, *Kirkus Reviews*, 1990.

WHAT DO FISH HAVE TO DO WITH ANYTHING?: Starred Review, *Publishers Weekly*; Starred Review, *School Library Journal*; Parent's Choice Silver Honor award, 1997.

WHEN I WAS YOUR AGE: Notable Children's Book in the Language Arts, National Council of Teachers of English, 1997.

"WHO WAS THAT MASKED MAN, ANYWAY?": American Library Association Notable 1993; Editors' Choice 1992, *Booklist*; One of the Best Books of 1992, *School Library Journal*; An American Bookseller Pick of the list, 1993; New York Public Library Children's Books: One Hundred Titles for Reading and Sharing, 1992; Starred Review, *Booklist*, 1992; Pointed Review, *Kirkus Reviews*, 1992; Starred Review, *Bulletin for the Center of Children's Books*, 1992; Starred Review, *School Library Journal*, 1992.

WINDCATCHER: One of the Best Books of the Year, Bank Street Teachers College, 1991.

WOLF RIDER: Young Adult Library Services Association Popular Paperbacks for Young Adults, 2001; *Booklist*, One of the Best Books of the Eighties, 1989; American Library Association Best Books for Young Adults, 1986; American Library Association/Young Adult Services Division Mystery Genre Book List, 1990; New York Public Library, Best Books, 1986; American Library Association/Young Adult Services Division Recommended Book for Reluctant Readers, 1986; Virginia Young Readers Award, 1990.

Avi. Autobiographical statement in *Twentieth-Century Children's Writers*. New York: St. Martin's, 1989, pp. 45–46.

Beck, Kathleen. Review of *Beyond the Western Sea, Book Two: Lord Kirkle's Money*. *Voice of Youth Advocates*, December 1996, p. 267.

Burns, Mary M. Review of *S.O.R. Losers*. *Horn Book*, January–February 1985, p. 49.

Fader, Ellen. Review of *The Barn*. *Horn Book*, January–February 1995, p. 57.

Review of *The Fighting Ground*. *Bulletin of the Center for Children's Books*, June 1984, p. 180.

Review of *The Man Who Was Poe*. *Bulletin of the Center for Children's Books*, October 1989, p. 27.

Review of *Nothing But the Truth*. *Publishers Weekly*, September 6, 1991, p. 105.

Phelan, Carolyn. Review of *Poppy*. *Booklist*, October 15, 1995, p. 402.

Review of *Poppy*. *Publishers Weekly*, August 21, 1995, p. 66.

Rochman, Hazel. Review of *Beyond the Western Sea, Book One: The Escape from Home*. *Booklist*, February 1, 1996, p. 930.

Roginski, Jim. *Behind the Covers: Interviews with Authors and Illustrators of Books for Children and Young Adults*, Libraries Unlimited, 1985, pp. 33–41.

Sutton, Roger. Review of *The Barn*. *Bulletin of the Center for Children's Books*, December 1994, p. 120.

Sutton, Roger. Review of *Tom, Babette & Simon*. *Bulletin of the Center for Children's Books*, July/August, 1995, p. 376.

Sutton, Roger. Review of *Beyond the Western Sea, Book One: The Escape from Home*. *Bulletin of the Center for Children's Books*, February 1996, p. 183.

Best Sellers, August 1979, pp. 165–66; June 1981, pp. 118–19; May 1982, p. 76.

Bulletin of the Center for Children's Books, July 1978, p. 170; July–August 1980, p. 206; June 1983; December 1986, p. 61; February 1986, p. 102; October 1987, p. 21; September 1988, p. 2; January 1996, p. 154; December 1996, p. 128.

English Journal, November 1981, p. 94.

Five Owls, January 1991, p. 56.

Horn Book, August 1979, p. 410; April 1980, pp. 169–70; October 1980, pp. 517–18; April 1981, p. 136; June 1981, pp. 297–98; August 1983, p. 439; June 1984, p. 325; January–February 1989, p. 65; January/February 1997, pp. 40–42.

Kirkus Reviews, January 1, 1997, p. 56.

Language Arts, October 1979, p. 822; November–December 1983, p. 1017; March 1985, p. 283.

New York Times Book Review, September 11, 1977; March 1, 1981, p. 24; January 1, 1995, p. 15.

Publishers Weekly, April 17, 1978, p. 78; December 5, 1980; January 30, 1981, p. 75; November 16, 1984, p. 65; December 26, 1986, p. 61; August 28, 1987, p. 81; September 14, 1990, p. 128; September 6, 1991, p. 105.

School Library Journal, March 1978, p. 124; May 1980, p. 64; November 1980, p. 68; September 1984, p. 125; October 1984, p. 164; December 1986, pp. 111–12; October 1987, p. 124; April 1994, p. 95; October 1996, p. 44.

Voice of Youth Advocates, August 1981, pp. 23–24; August 1982, p. 27; December 1984, pp. 261–62; February 1985, p. 321; February 1989, p. 293.

Avi. "All That Glitters," *Horn Book*, September–October, 1987, pp. 569–576.

Avi. "*Boston Globe-Horn Book* Award Acceptance Speech," *Horn Book*, January–February, 1992, p. 24–27.

Avi. "Curriculum Administrator Talks with Avi," *Curriculum Administrator*, Vol. 31, Issue 3, October 1996.

Avi. "On Historical Fiction," *Children's Book Council*, Author/Illustrator Archives, *www.cbcbooks.org*.

Avi. "The True Confessions of Charlotte Doyle," *Horn Book*, Vol. 68, Issue 1, January 1992.

Avi (with Betty Miles). "School Visits: The Author's Viewpoint," *School Library Journal*, January 1987, p. 21.

Benson, Sonia. "Avi," *Something about the Author*, Vol. 71. Farmington Hills, MI: Gale, 1992, pp. 7–15.

Bloom, Susan P., and Cathryn M. Mercier. *Presenting Avi*. New York: Twayne Publishers, 1997.

Bray, Donna. "Avi," *Horn Book*, July/August 2003, pp. 415–18.

Broderick, Kathleen. "Talking With Avi," *Book Links*, March 1997, pp. 56–58.

Brooks, Kathleen. "The Truth Will Not Set You Free If You Never Have A Chance To Speak, Or A Contradiction In Terms," *The Alan Review*, Winter 1996.

Cart, Michael. "Breakfast Serials," *Booklist*, January 1, 1999, Vol. 95, issue 9–10, pp. 846–48.

Cooper, Ilene. "Avi," *Booklist*, May 15, 2002, p. 1609.

Eftekhar, Judy. "The Transformation of Charlotte Doyle," *Writing*, Vol. 25, Issue 5, February/March 2003.

Harvey, Mary. "Advice from Avi," *Scholastic Scope*, Vol. 51, Issue 11, January 24, 2003.

Minarik, B. A. "Author Profile Avi," *Book Report*, Vol. 10, Issue 5, March/April 1992.

Milner Halls, Kelly. "The Magic of Avi," *Smart Writers*, May 2004, *www.smartwriters.com*.

Markham, Lois. *Avi*. Santa Barbara, CA: The Learning Works, 1996.

Sommers, Michael. *Avi*. New York: Rosen Publishing Group, 2004.

Winarski, Diana L. "Avi on Fiction," *Teaching K–8*, September 1997, pp. 62–64.

Benson, Sonia. "Avi," *Something about the Author,* Vol. 71, Gale, 1992, pp. 7–15.

Bloom, Susan P., and Cathryn M. Mercier. *Presenting Avi*. New York: Twayne Publishers, 1997.

Bray, Donna. "Avi," *Horn Book*, July/August 2003, pp. 415–18.

Cooper, Ilene. "Avi," *Booklist*, May 15, 2002, p.1609.

Eftekhar, Judy. "The Transformation of Charlotte Doyle," *Writing*, Vol. 25, Issue 5, February/March 2003.

Markham, Lois. *Avi*. Santa Barbara, CA: The Learning Works, 1996.

Minarik, B. A. "Author Profile Avi," *Book Report*, Vol. 10, Issue 5, March/April 1992.

Milner Halls, Kelly. "The Magic of Avi," *Smart Writers*, May 2004, *www.smartwriters.com*.

Sommers, Michael. *Avi*. New York: Rosen Publishing Group, 2004.

www.avi-writer.com
  [Avi's Website]

www.breakfastserials.com
  [Breakfast Serials web site, founded by Avi in 1996]

www.webenglishteacher.com/avi.html
  [A list of teacher resources for Avi's books]

www.cbcbooks.org
  [Avi, "On Historical Fiction," Children's Book Council, Author/Illustrator Archives]

MARGARET SPEAKER YUAN is the author of *Agnes de Mille: Dancer* (Chelsea House, 1990) and of three books about world landmarks: *Royal Gorge Bridge* (Blackbirch Press, 2003); *London Tower Bridge* (Blackbirch Press, 2004); and *Arc de Triomphe* (Blackbirch Press, 2004). She is the executive director of the Bay Area Independent Publishers Association, a nonprofit organization that provides educational seminars on publishing in the San Francisco Bay Area. She teaches art to children with learning disabilities as well as writing classes for both adults and children.